THE SOLESMES METHOD

THE SOLESMES METHOD

Its Fundamental Principles
and
Practical Rules of Interpretation

by

DOM JOSEPH GAJARD

TRANSLATED BY

R. Cecile Gabain

1959

THE LITURGICAL PRESS
Collegeville, Minnesota

FOREWORD

The following pages merely reproduce a series of articles which appeared in the *Revue Grégorienne* during the year 1950 under the title "Le Chant Grégorien et la Méthode de Solesmes." They make up the text of a lecture given in the Cathedral of Mexico on November 21, 1949, during the first Mexican Inter-American Congress on Sacred Music.[1]

The Congress, organized primarily for the benefit of Church musicians of the two Americas, had set itself a definitely practical task. Its object was to promote the restoration of sacred music on the American continent in accordance with the instructions of the latest Roman Pontiffs by pooling the ideas and efforts of all concerned. I had, nevertheless, the exceptional honor of being invited to attend the Congress in order to give a clear account of the Solesmes Method and, in a way, officially to explain this Method, which has been adopted almost universally throughout Mexico. I was asked to define it as it has emerged from the work of restoration on melody, rhythm, and paleography which has been carried on at Solesmes for nearly a century. Or, to put it differently, I was asked to show on what fundamental principles this Method is based, and also to give the practical rules for singing which are the outcome of these principles.

In spite of the very generous amount of time allotted to me, only a brief outline of the subject was possible, i.e., a survey of the peaks, a series of "chapter headings," all of which needed to be elaborated. The lecture itself has been published in the beautiful commemorative book of the Congress, lavishly produced by the Central Commission of Sacred Music of Mexico. It is the same text which is given here, as it appeared in the *Revue Grégorienne*, except for a few items of purely topical or local interest, and with the addition of some notes on the rules concerning style.

It struck me that here was a good opportunity for drawing up a sort of catalog or summary of the principal rules which are the

[1] See *Revue Grégorienne* (1950), pp. 219–232.

basis of the Solesmes Method. So often we are asked: "In what particular way can Dom Mocquereau's Method be recognized? How does it differ from others, and in particular from that of Dom Pothier? What is your 'secret'? What exactly must one do to sing as you think is right?" This little book is intended to provide a clear and succinct answer to these questions.

Part I, which is theoretical, sets forth what I would call the principles that constitute the Method of Solesmes. It gives a true description of it and shows how it may be distinguished from what it is not and the solid foundation on which it rests.

Part II, which is more definitely practical, gives the actual rules for singing, rules which are the logical outcome of these first and general principles. These rules may be divided into two categories: those which govern the technique of rhythm and those which affect style. The former survey in detail the interplay of the mechanism of rhythm and set forth the laws which govern its harmonious working in the rhythmical synthesis and in the unity of the piece when considered as a whole. These laws are the very foundation of any objective interpretation and cannot be ignored without the whole structure of a piece being undermined and its artistic value lost. They affect, moreover, not only Gregorian chant, but are applicable, at least in some degree, to every musical performance worthy of the name. They include accurate time-values, the progressive grouping of the single beat into compound beats, and of these into composite rhythms, clauses, phrases, periods, etc.

The remaining rules, which are complementary to the former, deal with style, i.e., with the various means of expression designed to temper the rigidity of any ill-mastered, materialistic or unskilled technique. They embody the lightness and suppleness which give the chant its spiritual character and create the work of art.

These rules concerning style are in their own way as important as the others. They are too often neglected and even ignored. Too often, also, even the rules concerning technique are given scant attention, to the great detriment of both the unity of the work and its musical quality, while those concerning style are completely by-passed. And so we hear the chant sung in a way that may be fairly correct, but is nevertheless material and cold, without soul or life, and that cannot translate the prayer which it is its function to express.

The objection might be raised that all these rules are not to be found in the chant manuscripts or in the treatises of the Middle

Ages. Obviously, musicology alone cannot have the last word; neither can paleography. True, they are witnesses of outstanding importance, but they are not the only ones. Since we speak of a chant which in its essence is Latin, Latin philology has an equal right to be heard, and so also, in the foremost rank, have the great laws which govern rhythm. The chants of the Divine Office are not museum pieces, carefully labelled and on view under glass cases. They are something truly living, and, above all, they are an integral part of "music" as such, which thereby loses none of its prerogatives. Musicology, paleography, and philology can only give us material facts; to become "music" they need to be imbued with rhythm and incorporated into a rhythmic whole.

Constant practice in choir may be of the greatest help. Dom Mocquereau acknowledges having discovered in this way much that was illuminating. The eminent musicologist Mgr. Anglès has also expressed the same opinion in the most explicit terms. He writes:

> Since Gregorian chant is prayer, in order to recover the rhythmic tradition, more is required than a collection of photographs and a work-table. The study of musical manuscripts must go hand in hand with regular practice in choir and with the daily carrying out of the liturgy. The musicologist may possess great historical and paleographical knowledge, yet if he does not also participate in the liturgical life and the divine worship of the Church, I do not think he will, in present times, be able to give enlightened guidance on the question of how to sing the Gregorian melodies.[2]

The reader will understand that we can give here only a brief and necessarily incomplete summary of the rules concerning rhythm and more especially of those concerning style. To be complete we should have had to develop our subject in a way that would be quite incompatible with the nature of this publication. We should thereby have defeated our aim, which is to give, not a complete treatise on Plainsong, but to provide, in an easily handled book of convenient size, a list of the principal rules to be followed in order to sing according to the Solesmes Method.

Neither will the reader find — at least not in most cases — any scientific proofs for what we say. If at times the application of our

---

[2] "Sul mensuralismo nelle melodie gregoriane" in *Der kultische Gesang der abendländischen Kirche*, p. 19.

principles raises a doubt, these principles have been set forth and fully explained in numerous articles in the *Revue Grégorienne*, and more especially in Dom Mocquereau's works, *Paléographie Musicale* and *Nombre Musical*, to which I need only refer my readers. I have had, moreover, to confine myself to merely a few explanations which, for the sake of clarity, were absolutely necessary.

This little book is not, therefore, in the usual sense of the word a "method," nor should it prevent anyone from having recourse to such methods for which it is not a substitute. Neither is it a treatise on rhythm as is, for instance, our *Notions sur la Rythmique Grégorienne*. It is merely a summary, with explanatory notes, of the theoretical and practical principles which underlie a good and intelligent rendering of the Gregorian melodies.

For a considerable time I had planned something of this kind, and my lecture at Mexico seems to provide the necessary material. In these pages I have summed up what I have learned during forty years of daily practice in choir and choir direction. Those who have stayed at Solesmes and paid us the honor of consulting us will not fail to recognize here the teaching that Dom Mocquereau and I have unceasingly given our guests and which finds expression in the singing of the monks. Moreover, these pages repeat, textually, what I have said elsewhere.

My one aim has been to give the code of rules which we have followed faithfully for more than half a century. These rules are the outcome of the enlightened work on rhythm and paleography by the one whom we revere as the head of the Solesmes school. I dedicate these lines to those who, throughout the world, wish to remain faithful to his teaching.

Although these principles as here stated may seem incomplete, they will, when applied, suffice to give the sacred melodies their full value. They will imbue them with warmth and life and the power of spiritual expression, and impart to them that character of both art and prayer which is the hallmark of the sung prayer of the Church.

CONTENTS

THE SOLESMES METHOD
PART I
FUNDAMENTAL PRINCIPLES

PART II

PRACTICAL RULES OF INTERPRETATION

A. Rules of Rhythmical Technique

B. Rules on Style

THE SOLESMES METHOD

PRELIMINARY OBSERVATIONS

The Most Important Attempts At Interpretation

The task of restoring the Gregorian melodies, begun approximately a century ago, has been long and arduous, and this fact is perhaps too little known. Much ground had to be covered, and for the workers who undertook this heavy task it meant starting from practically zero as regards both melody and rhythm. Great demands were made on their time and patience as they gropingly felt their way toward the full light. This was particularly the case in everything concerning rhythm, about which information was very deficient.

Many systems have been put forward, most often independently of one another. They have met with varying success; for some, failure was to be expected.

I wish here to explain the method of interpretation established by Dom Mocquereau, which is known as the "Solesmes Method." In order to leave the reader in no doubt as to what characterizes this method, I think it will be useful to first summarize the principal attempts at interpretation which have been made and which are now but faint landmarks on the long road which has been covered. In doing this I shall not attempt to refute them, but, by a process of elimination, I shall remove obstructions and thus pave the way for my thesis, so that it may, by contrast, stand out the more clearly.

The methods of interpretation so far given to the public can be broadly divided into two categories: those of the mensuralists or partisans of so-called measured rhythm, and those of the partisans of so-called free rhythm.

Mensuralism

Mensuralists are usually partisans of at least some kind of fixed time. This system was in a way the logical outcome of the prevailing mistaken ideas on the very nature of rhythm. If, as was often taken for granted, the words "rhythm" and "measure" describe the same reality, it follows that without a fixed measure there can be no rhythm. Thence the necessity of rediscovering some kind of measure or set time in Gregorian chant in order to instil rhythm into it.

This was certainly a crude error and the outcome of a mistaken conception of rhythm which had been in vogue for a considerable length of time. Measure and rhythm, even in the most elementary sense of the words, are, of course, specifically different realities.

They have this in common: each is made up of a succession of sound elements or undulations which are characterized by the return of a "marked beat." This, unfortunately, has too often been looked upon as the strong or loud beat, whereas it has nothing to do with volume of sound. I shall return later to these elementary facts.

What specifically characterizes measure in music of the classical period is the regular or isochronous return (i.e., at equal intervals of time) of this marked beat, as in our measures with a fixed time signature. In contrast to this — and the distinction is of capital importance — Gregorian chant allows the free return of its marked beat at equal or unequal intervals of time, according to the composer's wish, and we have bars with two or three beats each, freely mixed.

Freely measured rhythm thus escapes from that mechanical restraint of a fixed measure which is merely a materializing of the infinitely more flexible laws of rhythm.

Embedded in the habits of contemporary music, most of which was in a fixed measure or apparently so (much more could be said about this), the mensuralists of the nineteenth century wished to give some rhythmical shape to the battered remains of Gregorian chant, which had survived the slow ravages of time. To achieve their end they could find nothing better than to inflict on the melodies a fixed measure or set pace. This they did in various ways.

a) Some, the pure mensuralists, insisted on arranging the plainsong melodies so that they had to fit willy-nilly into the framework of a set time with a single time signature. I will quote only one of the most representative of them, Father Dechevrens, S.J. Here, for instance, is the *Asperges* [1] arranged in two time.

Obviously, the poor melodies could only react unfavorably to such Procrustean treatment which had been inflicted upon them because of an assumption and was without any justification.

b) Others have been less ruthless. They did not subject the Gregorian melodies to a fixed time but to the law of quantity which underlies the former. Houdard is a case in point with his theory of the "neum-beat." In this scheme, each neum, whether short or long, is given the value of one beat represented by a quarter-note. Here, for example, is the same *Asperges* arranged as it would be by Houdard:

[1] *Composition littéraire et composition musicale, t. II:* "Rythme Grégorien," p. 166.

Note also particularly the Alleluia *Justus germinabit*, which Houdard must have valued highly because he quotes it in at least two of his books and speaks of it as "one of the most graciously inspired of the Gregorian melodies known to us." [2]

Alle- lú-   ia.

In spite of the fine commentaries of an apparently scientific and paleographic nature that have been written in support of these absurdities, they remain, nevertheless, a challenge, not only to the science of neums, but also to the most elementary common sense.

c) Dom Jeannin, a Benedictine monk of Hautecombe, without going so far, maintained that the chant required some kind of "metrical framework," [3] because he was convinced that "in the golden age of Plainsong, the melodies were given some definite form of time, although this was very different from the various systems proposed by the mensuralists." [4] His aim was to uphold his thesis that the Latin accent is long and on the down-beat. He therefore set about reducing every long note of the manuscripts to the value of a quarter-note.[5]

Qui   sí-   tit   vé- ni-   at et   bí- bat :   et de

vén-tre   é-   jus   flú- ent á-quae   ví- vae.

[2] *Le rythme du chant dit grégorien* (1898), p. 216.

[3] *Mélodies liturgiques syriennes et chaldéennes* (Paris, 1924), p. 198. Reproduced by Dom Mocquereau in *Monographie VII*, "Examen des critiques dirigées par Dom Jeannin contre l'École de Solesmes" (Tournai, 1926), p. 15.

[4] *Mél. Lit.*, p. 166; *Monographie VII*, p. 17.

[5] *Mél. Lit.*, p. 186; *Monographie VII*, p. 70.

And here is the same theory applied to ornate chant.

As Dom Mocquereau has said, "Dom Jeannin's theory is directly opposed to that of Houdard. The latter unreasonably restricts all neums and their value, whereas Dom Jeannin stretches them inordinately."[6]

d) Even Dom Ferretti, the second director of the Pontifical School of Sacred Music in Rome, had a leaning toward mensuralism. Well versed in meter, he had as a youth a special liking for the works of medieval writers. He tried to discover in the Gregorian melodies the feet of classical Latin meter. He expounded this in his book *Il Cursu Metrico*, but the book met with no success; it remained unread and the enlightened author, recognizing his mistake, rallied wholeheartedly to the teaching of Solesmes. Proof of this is given in his *Grammaire du Chant grégorien* and in his teaching at the Pontifical Institute in Rome.

I will not dwell any longer on mensuralist theories except to recall the name of Dr. Pierre Wagner, who also to some extent went in for mensuralism, but with this distinction that he adopted a "rhythmical interpretation for syllabic chants and a metrical interpretation for melismatic chants."

All these systems are, in fact, based upon pure imagination. What stands out as most absurd is that, although they all contradict one another, they are all based on the same texts by medieval writers, whose clarity they all extol and whose obvious meaning each one claims to know. This in itself is a condemnation of one and all. In a course of lectures on modality and rhythm given at the Pontifical Institute in Rome and since published in roneotype (*Appunti di teoria superiore gregoriana*, Rome, 1936–37), Dom

[6] *Monographie VII*, p. 22.

Ferretti has made the most detailed, clear, and circumstantial criticism that has so far been written of both the mensuralist theories and of the texts on which they are based. Because he had believed in them for so long, his estimate of the medieval writers is all the more precious and authoritative. I remember him saying to me in his cell at Solesmes: "There is nothing to be gained from the writers of the Middle Ages — nothing, nothing, nothing!"

Moreover, the authors of all these systems had difficulty enough in getting them accepted even in their own lifetime and in their immediate surroundings. Except for a few that have lingered on, they have not survived the men who created them. Now, for all practical purposes, they are dead, and so we may leave them to sleep in peace. *Requiescant in pace*!

Free Rhythm

In complete contrast to mensuralism, which seeks to reduce Gregorian rhythm to a more or less fixed time, there has arisen the theory of so-called free rhythm, which has conquered most, if not all, those who practice the chant today.

This theory takes two forms which, although not directly opposed to each other, differ considerably in their varying degrees of exactness and by some marked characteristics. They are: the theory of *free speech rhythm*, which has also been named Dom Pothier's theory, and the theory of *free musical rhythm*, which is that of Dom Mocquereau.

Strange as it may seem on a first approach, both theories are upheld by Benedictines and both come from Solesmes. This may easily give rise to misunderstanding. Since differences of opinion now exist (and in a definitely weakened form) only between the partisans of one or the other of these two theories of free rhythm, it is important that we should clearly define each one and describe exactly what is and what is not the teaching of Solesmes. We are now coming to grips with the problem.

FREE SPEECH RHYTHM

The theory of so-called free rhythm was not born of an *a priori* idea but of a fact: this was the manner of chanting which Dom Guéranger gave to his monks. Dom Guéranger had just restored

Benedictine life in France in the Priory of Solesmes. To his contemplative monks he gave as their primary activity the *Opus Dei*, i.e., the most perfect celebration of the liturgy, as explicitly formulated in the Rule of St. Benedict: *Nihil operi Dei praeponatur*. They had, therefore, to sing.

In spite of the mutilated condition of what remained of the old Gregorian art, Dom Guéranger, with his sense of "catholicity," foresaw what the sung prayer of the Church might be, and he seemed instinctively to realize all that was true and pure, holy and divine in these incomparable melodies. And so, until it was possible for the melodies to be restored to their original and authentic form, he turned his attention to improving the rendering of the chant by putting a stop to the rough treatment and hammering out of the notes then in common practice everywhere. With the help of reading and observation, by thought and discussion, with the aid, too, of good taste, and quite evidently with help from Heaven, he managed to give the monks' singing a natural flowing pace, an unaffected spontaneity which very soon charmed all those who came as guests to the monastery. One of these, Chanoine Gontier of Le Mans, saw in this, as it were, a "revelation." With helpful advice from Dom Guéranger, he made an attempt to formulate and codify the principles upon which the monks' singing was based in his *Méthode raisonnée de plainchant*, published in 1859.

In this *Method*, M. Gontier deliberately broke away from all the false theories which the would-be reformers had up till then imported into Gregorian chant from contemporary music. He abandoned both measure or a fixed time and proportional length of sounds, and taught the freedom of Gregorian rhythm, the indivisibility of the primary beat and the outstanding part played by the Latin accent in the formation of rhythm. Plainsong he defined as "a modulated recitation in which the notes have an undefined time value, and in which the rhythm, which is essentially free, is that of speech."[7] And he summed up his teaching thus: "The rule which stands out above all others is that, except in the case of pure melody, the chant should be intelligent, well-accentuated, well-phrased reading, in which the laws of quantity are observed."[8]

In a flash the Gregorian phrase had once again found its wings. Freed from the chains that had held it captive, it could now spring

[7] *Méthode raisonnée de plainchant*, chap. I, p. 1.
[8] *Op. cit.*, chap. II, p. 14.

forth and hover on the heights. Obviously all this was vague and inadequate. Nevertheless, the seed had been sown and would bear fruit.

Mgr. Rousseau has written: "M. Gontier's work was truly the first valuable contribution to the rhythmical restoration of the chant. It may justly be considered as the immediate precursor of Dom Pothier's celebrated *Les Mélodies Grégoriennes*, and in it the fundamental axioms of the Solesmes Method are clearly formulated." [9] This truly was the first landmark in the restoration of the chant.[10]

In his *Mélodies Grégoriennes*, written in collaboration with Dom Jausions and published in 1880, Dom Pothier merely confirmed the principles which had been embodied twenty years earlier in Chanoine Gontier's book. The question of neums was approached in an entirely new way and showed definite progress. Medieval writers were carefully studied with remarkable penetration and their works were commented upon in masterly fashion. Dom Pothier gleaned as much as possible from them, and on this point his book remains as young as ever. The question of rhythm was also more fully developed. Laws on the rhythm of speech were better defined, and, in particular, the nature and role of the Latin accent were made to stand out clearly.

"This book," Dom Mocquereau tells us, "met with unexpected success. It was translated into German and Italian, and revolutionized the interpretation of Plainsong. All writers of new textbooks rallied to the teaching of the Solesmes monk." [11]

At the time of publication of this theoretical treatise and, in 1883, of the Roman Gradual, Dom Ferretti wrote: "*Speech rhythm* became common usage outside Solesmes and was looked upon as a musical dogma." [12]

In what exactly does speech rhythm consist? What are its fundamental principles? Although Dom Pothier himself never officially formulated them, I think that what follows will give a fair description.

1) Exclusion of all measure or fixed time or of a regular metrical framework.

[9] *L'Ecole Grégorienne de Solesmes*, p. 44.
[10] For an account of free speech rhythm, see "Rythme oratoire et Rythme musical," in *Rev. Grég.* (1928), pp. 144–150, and *Les débuts de la restauration grégorienne à Solesmes* (Solesmes, 1939), pp. 9–19.
[11] *Revue Grégorienne* (1920), p. 185.
[12] *Appunti di Teoria superiore gregoriana*, p. 362.

2) Assimilation to the free rhythm of speech. In this the sounds as well as the syllables have an undefined time-value, of which the proportion is determined by natural instinct without any set rules, as Dom Pothier himself wrote: "It is a number or proportion which exists in speech without being apparent; one *feels* it and on hearing it one is charmed by it, but one cannot say exactly what it is." This fundamental *lack of clear definition*, this *vagueness* or approximation is what primarily characterizes Gregorian speech rhythm.

3) Exclusive importance given in syllabic chant to the tonic accent of the word and, in ornate chant, to the first note of each neum. This then becomes equivalent to the accented syllable of a word and is itself accented. All of which amounts to saying that rhythm is based not on quantity as laid down by the mensuralists but on *stress* or *volume* of sound. In short, rhythm was in practice considered as being a succession of strong and weak beats, if not by Dom Pothier himself (he rather wavered on this point), at least by his most accredited disciples.

4) Preponderance given to the words rather than to the melody, whether ornate or syllabic, or, in other words, subordination of the melody to the words.

5) Finally, attention is almost exclusively directed to the important divisions of phrasing — to groups, clauses and phrases. "Number and proportion," Dom Pothier tells us, "must make themselves felt chiefly at the beginning and end of these divisions. All that is required for what comes in between, i.e., for the middle of phrases, is that nothing should shock or offend the ear in the succession of sounds. There need be no searching after superfluous rhythmical perfection."

To sum up: *rhythm based on stress* or *volume* of sound with *undefined time-values* as in speech, in which the *tonic accent plays the principal part*, which part is felt only *at cadences.*

We have now reached the crucial point which must be clearly seen if we are to understand the position taken up by Dom Mocquereau and his school with regard to Dom Pothier's theory. This theory most certainly contains much that is true, but its upholders were unable to avoid exaggerations and, in consequence, even serious mistakes. Without realizing it, Dom Pothier in wishing to avoid one danger ran into another, and, because he had not got to the root of things, from a true principle (the liberty of rhythm) he drew a wrong conclusion (its lack of clear definition).

It was this that led his disciple Dom Mocquereau to erect that vast edifice which, it must be recognized, has completely renewed the whole theory of rhythm itself. In explaining this theory and the well-founded facts on which it is based, I shall at the same time, without even having to mention them again by name, make clear the deficiencies of "speech rhythm."

FREE MUSICAL RHYTHM

Coming from a musical family, Dom Mocquereau was endowed with the finest artistic sensibility. He was himself an excellent musician and brought to the monastery the fruits of a thorough musical education. Moreover, he was young, vigorous, capable of an enormous output and was a hard and steady worker. He had, therefore, all that was needed for success in the task to be assigned to him. By nature opposed to half measures, he always went straight for his goal; not anyone or anything could make him swerve from the path which he recognized as leading to the truth. He also had great humility and, devoid of any kind of personal vanity, was always ready to efface himself and spontaneously to accept anything he considered to be objectively true.

He was made an associate of Dom Pothier, and, in spite of a positive dislike for Gregorian chant, which he then regarded as uninteresting and of no musical value, he worked with him and held him in great affection all his life. Dom Mocquereau has sometimes been accused of opposing his master. This is gross calumny, for, on the contrary, he at that time devoted himself wholeheartedly to defending Dom Pothier's work, especially his *Liber Gradualis* of 1883, which had given rise to violent controversy. It was actually in giving him this support that he came to perfect Dom Pothier's achievements and very soon to surpass him.

And this is how it came about. From the first, Dom Mocquereau had realized that Gregorian chant, by the very form of its composition, was in open conflict with the then accepted tenets of the art of music. For anyone brought up on the theory of the stressed or loud first beat and a theory of rhythm based on volume of sound — the theory held by Dom Pothier — the frequent recurrence of final syllables of words or even of weak penultimate dactylic syllables laden with a wealth of neums, coming after an accented syllable on only one note, created an enigma which even shocked him.

And yet, before long, his experience in choir helped him to modify this attitude. He very soon began to find great beauty in these chants and "allowed himself to be captivated by their charm."

Nevertheless, he was now faced with a problem which must inevitably present itself to anyone with an open mind. How could this chant, which was in contradiction to the generally accepted laws of music, give such real satisfaction to the most critical and sensitive ear? And if so, did not this mean that these so-called laws needed to be revised and carefully investigated?

It became clear to him that such an examination was necessary. Must the tonic accent necessarily coincide with the down-beat? This question had to be answered. A musician first, he was wise enough to put his trust in music and to let himself be rocked by the gentle but very clear rhythm of the melody without, at this stage, bothering about the accompanying words.

The internal criticism of the melodies which he attempted in Volumes III and IV of his *Paléographie Musicale*, in order to support from within Dom Pothier's paleographic work of restoration, gradually revealed to him the principal laws which govern the composition of a Gregorian melody. And he noticed in particular the important but limited role of the Latin tonic accent. It became clear that in many cases the melody took on a character of its own in which the tonic accent no longer played quite so important and unique a part as had hitherto been assigned to it. Nor did it always occupy that position in the rhythm which had been regarded as sacrosanct. The music outweighed the words. Here was an illustration of the old saying: *Musica non subjacet regulis Donati.*

But then, what part did the words play in Gregorian rhythm? What in itself is the tonic accent? What is its role in relation to the word? How is it related to rhythm? This difficult problem presupposed that another problem, equally complicated, had already been solved, namely, what is rhythm in itself, independently of the words? What is an ictus? How is it related to each of those qualities which constitute and are inseparable from the production of a musical sound — volume, pitch, and duration? All these questions needed to be answered.

Dom Mocquereau undertook the task with courage. He first looked to the musical facts themselves: to Greco-Latin poetry (which was also music), to Saint Gregory's melodies, to Palestrinian polyphony, and to the works of our great classical composers. He then turned to theorists of all ages, to those of Greece, of the Middle Ages, and of our own time, searching for clear information on rhythm, its fundamental laws and development and its various

forms. He then faced the second and perhaps more difficult aspect
of the problem: the Latin language. Here, his study of Latin grammarians and modern philologists confirmed, point by point, and
in a wonderful way, the conclusions of a musical nature which he
had reached. Thus, internal analysis of the Gregorian melodies and
both musical and Latin philology justified and scientifically proved
the rightness of his conception of rhythm, which, from the start,
good taste and his artistic sense had suggested to him.[13] This was
that rhythm is based on music and not on speech, is independent
of volume of sound or stress, with the Latin accent sometimes on
the up-beat, sometimes on the down-beat, according to the requirements of the melodic line or the neumatic notation. "Music"
had been a wise counsellor; she had proved worthy of the trust
he had placed in her.[14]

This synthesis, it must be understood, only emerged gradually
after much groping. Dom Mocquereau first developed it in the
seventh volume of *La Paléographie Musicale*, and then, and deservedly so, more methodically and comprehensively in the two
volumes of his *Nombre Musical Grégorien*.

This was the theory of so-called free musical rhythm, or, as officially described by the author himself in the title of his book, of
"*nombre musical grégorien*," a happy choice of words as they adequately define it. "*Nombre*," or number (Latin *numerus*), because
this is the classical Latin term used to describe in one word rhythm
which is free.. "*Musical*," because instead of the vagueness of
speech rhythm, we get clearly defined rhythm in its most perfect
form, which is musical rhythm; also, because the rhythm here is
determined far more by the melody than by the words. "*Grégorien*," because these laws are in the main peculiar to the liturgical
melodies of the Latin Church, named "Gregorian" in memory of
Saint Gregory the Great.

Such is the theory generally known either as the "Method of
Dom Mocquereau" or as the "Method of Solesmes." In the following treatise I shall confine myself entirely to describing this
Method, its underlying principles, and the practical rules of interpretation which are derived from these principles.

---

[13] J. Combarieu, *Théorie du rythme et essai sur l'archéologie musicale au
XIX.* siècle, pp. 178–180.

[14] Cf. "Le Nombre Musical Grégorien" in *Rev. Grég.* (1927), pp. 202–206
(reproduced in *Monographie XII*, pp. 5–10); "Les débuts de la restauration,"
pp. 23–40.

THE SOLESMES METHOD

Free Musical Rhythm

PART I

FUNDAMENTAL PRINCIPLES

What are the fundamental principles of the Solesmes Method? Here they are, and merely to state them will show how greatly they differ from those of speech rhythm.

1) Gregorian rhythm is specifically of a *musical* nature and is not the rhythm of speech.

2) Every step in the rhythmical synthesis is clearly defined: (a) the indivisible primary beat; (b) elementary rhythms and binary and ternary compound beats; (c) composite rhythms.

3) There is complete independence of rhythm and stress.

4) Hence there is complete independence of the rhythmic ictus and the tonic accent, and rhythm which is entirely free in its movement.

5) The words are subordinate to the melody.

6) Traditional interpretation and expression are followed. These are based on the concordant evidence of the oldest manuscripts.

I shall take up each of these points briefly, since I cannot give them the full treatment they require here.

1. THE INHERENTLY MUSICAL NATURE OF GREGORIAN RHYTHM

At the very beginning of the second volume of the *Nombre Musical,* Dom Mocquereau described at some length the "consider-

15

able and important differences" which exist between the art of speech and the art of music, in spite of their affinity on certain points.[1]

If we approach the subject from the *melodic* point of view, we find that speech has its own tonality and melody which are confined to no set scale and move by a series of indefinite "continuous" steps, entirely according to the choice, taste, and art of the orator, who as a soloist, does not need to bother about the blending of voices. Melody, on the other hand, is not merely declaimed, it is sung. This fact alone means that it no longer depends solely on the taste of the singer, but that it is subject to the inexorable laws of the diatonic scale, which must be faithfully observed, more especially when there is group singing.

From the *rhythmic* point of view, also, declamation has its own speed, its own gait or manner of moving, which the orator is free to hasten, rush, slow down, or moderate according to his own feelings or to those he wishes to arouse in his audience. Although he may be subject to the great laws which govern articulation, accentuation, and breathing, yet he may apply them with the greatest freedom. He is, I repeat, a soloist. In singing, on the contrary, and especially in group singing, this irregularity in delivery must give way to a more stable pace. Syllables and notes tend to broaden and to become equalized, and their time-value is more clearly felt and recognized. Thanks to melodic cadences, the rhythmic divisions are better outlined and more defined, not to speak of the many instances where the melody stretches both syllables and words and imposes upon them its own purely musical rhythm.

"It is," says Dom Mocquereau, "as impossible to adapt the complete rhythmic freedom of oratory, with its license and intangible range of expression, to Gregorian chant as it is to apply to it the vague melodic intonations of speech." Moreover, rhythm, to be free, need not be vague and indefinite; in fact, the contrary is the case.

2. RHYTHM MUST NECESSARILY BE WELL DEFINED

The complete assimilation of Gregorian rhythm to the rhythm of recitation and speech as a reaction against its assimilation to the rhythm of poetry and of so-called strictly measured music obvi-

[1] *Nombre Musical*, t. II, pp. 54–58. Cf. "Rythme oratoire et Rythme musical," *Rev. Grég.* (1928), pp. 185–189.

ously comes from confusing the terms "well-defined rhythm" and "measured rhythm," [2] and from a lack of understanding of the true nature of rhythm itself. I must make this clear.

So-called measured rhythm implies (a) rhythm which is well defined; (b) rhythm which is not only well defined but to which a strictly metrical framework has been added. This framework is characterized by the return of a marked beat (call it by what name you will) at predetermined set intervals of time and, except in the case of an expressive change of speed, with isochronous regularity. This is the typical rhythm of our marching songs.

But rhythm may be well defined without of necessity being molded into a predetermined metrical framework. The rhythmical elements which make up a musical phrase should be clearly defined and outlined, but need not be divided into measures of equal length. What is required is that, although its recurs without isochronous regularity, the existence of the marked beat can be recognized and that it be perceptible to the ear.

Examples of this abound everywhere and are to be found even in ancient poetry. In his introduction to the *Nombre Musical* (pp. 1–40) in his study of asynartetic verses (which are made up of two clauses, each with a different rhythm), of logaoedic verses (in which a clause is made up of different kinds of feet), and of dochmiacs, Dom Mocquereau shows how poetry itself could and in fact often did make itself infinitely flexible so as to come, as it were, near to prose. And yet it does this without breaking the laws of prosody. The word "logaoedic," by its very etymology (*logos-aoide* = discourse-song) is suggestive, since it signifies that approximation of poetry and prose which allows language to derive something from both: from verse the prosodic exactness of the feet used; from prose the freedom with which they are coordinated.

And what of our own contemporary music, in which measures of two, three, four, five or more beats to the bar are so readily mixed? Such a procedure may at times degenerate into creating works which are weak and shapeless; nevertheless, its use remains a recognized fact and does at least testify to the need felt by our young composers to break away from the convention of a "set measure" in order to give themselves up to a freer conception of "rhythm."

Rhythm is, therefore, independent of measure or the bar, al-

[2] The reader is here referred to "Rythme oratoire et Rythme musical," *Rev. Grég.* (1928), pp 189–191, 224–229; (1929) pp. 96–101, 110–148.

though it is based on number and is, according to Maurice Emmanuel, the "regulator of time-values." Rhythm is in the first place a matter of relationship, "order in movement," as it has so rightly been defined, and, in movement, there is no need to take steps of necessarily equal length.

But if the Platonic definition in no way implies the idea of materialistic, isochronous measure, it does include the idea of something well defined. It is not enough to state, as I have done, that rhythm without a set measure *may* be well defined; the truth is that rhythm *must* be so if it is to be truly rhythm.

When we say "order," we do in fact mean hierarchy of exact relationship between *well-defined* objective elements, for there can be no order where things are vague and nebulous. So long as beings are not constituted with their own clearly circumscribed individuality, there can be no true relationship between them, still less can there be ordered relationship. So, in strictly logical terms, either rhythm is well defined or there is no rhythm.

What specifically distinguishes so-called free rhythm from measured rhythm is not more or less exactness but the repetition of the marked beat or rhythmic touching-point either at fixed or at undetermined intervals of time. In each case we have a relationship between well-defined and clear elements. In measured rhythm there is complete quantitative equality between all these elements and an isochronous return of the marked beat according to pre-established convention. In free rhythm, however, constituent elements are of unequal length and we get a freely recurring marked beat, or, in simpler terms, a mixture of binary and ternary feet.

That is why all music which is basically rhythmic (rhythm, according to ancient writers, was the "male" element in music) rests upon well-defined values. And it is between these varying and exact values that there arise relationships which are themselves exact and which constitute musical rhythm.

That is also why, as M. D. Laloy justly remarks in his admirable study of Aristoxenus of Tarentum,[3] speech, or better still, recitation, is not truly rhythm; it can only approximate rhythm as if by analogy. After speaking of rhythmical modulations, he says:

> No doubt some will object to such a theory because it defines the rhythm of speech and not that of poetry. *But this is only playing with words.* The rhythm of speech is vague and undetermined, *a mere outline of rhythm*, because in it there

[3] A disciple of Aristotle, born 354 B.C.

is no definite relationship between the syllables. The rhythm of poetry is on the contrary exact, because in it each group is split up into equal and unequal beats between which the relationship can immediately be recognized, and the words of which we were speaking are rhythmical words, dactyls, iambs or paeons, that is to say, they form *well-defined* measures of two, three and five beats. The variety of these measures enlivens free rhythm without in any way diminishing its clarity.[4]

M. Laloy often returns to this idea, and his work on the great rhythmician of antiquity, written without any thought of system or school, is very well informed and authoritative. For him, obviously, as soon as music intervenes, rhythm loses the vagueness of speech and becomes strictly "musical," that is to say, well defined. Moreover, Gregorian chant is music.

If space allowed, we could show how prose itself originally uneven and without form, very gradually borrowed the metrical feet from poetry which, in its own way, it adapted freely as if concealing them in the flow of speech. Rhythm thus reached its perfection and became free, varied, ample, and harmonious, at the same time avoiding, according to M. Croiset's apt description, "even the appearance of mechanism."[5] There is no lack of witnesses from the past: Dionysius of Halicarnasse, Cicero, Quintilian, to mention only a few. In connection with Dionysius of Halicarnasse, we need only recall the suggestive titles of the last two chapters of his classical work on the *Arrangement of words*: "How a poem or an ode may be likened to beautiful prose" and "How a piece of writing in prose may be likened to a beautiful poem or a beautiful ode."

How can rhythm be made so well defined as to be perfect and musical? To achieve this end, rhythm needs to be felt not only at the beginning and end of each division, i.e., it must not only ensure some proportion between the divisions of a phrase or distribute each of the cadences in an harmonious and "numbered" manner; it must penetrate *the very texture of the literary or melodic material*, and it must make itself felt everywhere, in the middle of phrases quite as much as at their beginning and end. In other words, it must regulate every step of the rhythmic movement, whether this be made up of equal or unequal beats, and the relationship between these should be immediately recognizable. Un-

[4] *Aristoxenus of Tarentum*, pp. 335–336.
[5] *Histoire de la littérature grecque* (Paris, 1887–99), t. IV, p. 11.

less these simple elements are present and clearly defined, there can be no true proportion, no order, no rhythm.

A final analysis will show that musical rhythm depends upon two elements which are vital to it: *a time-unit,* the single beat, and the *grouping of these single beats into definite entities* — compound beats, which themselves combine to form composite rhythms, groups, clauses, phrases, etc.

a) The single or primary beat

As a basis we have a time-unit, the primary beat, rightly described by M. Laloy as "indivisible, and thus defined because of its very indivisibility." And he adds: "The primary beat is the beat which can take only one syllable, one note, one figure." [6]

All authors who have written on classical rhythm are agreed on this point. Here is what M. Maurice Emmanuel has so aptly written on the subject: [7]

> The principles on which Greco-Roman rhythm is founded differ completely from those which govern ours. We split up a "large" unit, which is the whole note. This is looked upon as the maximum duration-value of which the divisions and the subdivisions into two's and three's are unlimited, their only limit being the practical realization of the generated speeds. The Greeks, on the contrary, started from a "small" unit, looked upon as the minimum duration-value, which was indivisible and could be applied to the most rapid musical sound, syllable or bodily movement, and they used far greater liberty in forming it into rhythmic groups than we dare take with our whole note "coinage." Thus our modern rhythmic unit is essentially *divisible*; that of the ancients was *multipliable* . . . and the latter was named "primary beat."

If the primary beat, as represented by the Gregorian note (whatever its form in the so-called square notation) is given the value of an eighth note, there will be no place for sixteenth or thirty-second notes, etc. This clearly defined primary beat is *the basis of the whole rhythmic structure,* the norm and criterion for all other units in the rhythmic whole.

And yet how often do our modern interpreters forget this fundamental principle? "It is," says M. Combarieu, "one of the chief characteristics of Gregorian chant, and the serenity and nobility of

[6] *Op. cit.,* pp. 295–296.
[7] *Histoire de la langue musicale,* pp. 110–111.

the chant depends in a large measure on the faithful observance of this law." [8] Gregorian rhythm is based on the indivisibility of the primary beat, just as the modality of the chant is based on the diatonic scale, on what might be called the "indivisibility of the tone." Neglect of one or the other of these principles inevitably leads to a travesty of the chant and is the negation of Gregorian art.

Obviously, the primary beat may vary in duration according to the piece sung. But "once the speed has been chosen," says M. Laloy, "the duration element is stabilized and the rhythm is then made up of beats which are clearly defined as regards their duration, number, relationship, and order of succession." [9]

b) The grouping of primary beats into compound beats

In practice, primary beats are grouped into binary and ternary compound beats. By "compound beat" I mean what musical terminology of today would perhaps describe as the "beat" or as a small measure in 2/8 or 3/8.

We have spoken of binary and ternary compound beats. We thus admit that there exists a rhythmical intermediary between the note and the group, an intermediary which is necessary and essential to the rhythm itself. This needs some further explanation.

Gregorian art cannot escape from a universal law which, without exception, governs all the arts of movement. Be it poetry or declamation, music, Gregorian chant, marching or dance movements, rhythm makes the same demands and must move by step. Like everything composite, it is made up of simple elements. This is a universal law from which nothing is exempt, not even the most beautiful lyrical outpourings. Rhythm which flows in that undefined element we call time can only be appreciated if it is measured out in small, simple movements which, as we have already said, can be easily perceived. Unlike that of the angels, the human mind cannot at once grasp a vast whole but must make use of the double process of analysis and synthesis.

"Every musical phrase," says M. Laloy, "is made up of rhythmical groups just as every spoken phrase is made up of words. We can perceive a rhythm only if it is split up into groups. This is a law peculiar to our understanding, from which there is no escape either in Gregorian chant or in modern music." [10]

[8] *Théorie du rythme*, p. 38.
[9] *Op. cit., ibid.*
[10] *Revue musicale* (Oct. 1903), p. 548.

"Through rhythm alone," says M. Combarieu, "the sound matter takes shape, and through rhythm it becomes a living organism,
an ordered and intelligible whole; and the mind of the listener,
instead of wandering at random, takes joy in itself as if in the revelation of its own eurhythmy." [11] This could not be better expressed.

Moreover, the rhythm of Plainsong is subject, like all other forms
of rhythm, to certain fundamental and universal laws from which,
as I have said, neither speech, music, nor the dance can be exempt.
We also have the testimony of the medieval musicologists. This,
Dom Mocquereau tells us, was so clear that mensuralists of today
need only to stretch its meaning in order to give to their own theories some appearance of sense.[12] *Veluti metricis pedibus cantilena
plaudatur . . . plaudam pedes . . . more metri diligenter men-
surandum sit . . .* etc. (Hucbald, 840–930). In his teaching,
Guido of Arezzo (1050) repeats this word for word.

It is on these texts that the mensuralists founded their theories,
but the mistake they made was to interpret them too literally.
What does not seem open to doubt is the existence in the Middle
Ages of these subdivisions, whatever their nature or duration. Let
us state once more: "It is the organizing, whether regular or free,
of these compound beats and not their presence or absence which
determines the specific differences between rhythm in a set measure and freely measured rhythm." All forms of rhythm can, in
fact, be reduced to two: (1) the measured form (*vincta*), in which
the movement is regularly binary or regularly ternary; (2) the
free form (*soluta*), in which the movement is irregular and free
and in which the binary and ternary beats succeed each other and
are harmoniously mingled.

The *vincta* form, which is smooth and measured, can be recognized by its regular pace, by the return of the ictus, touching-
points, or marked beats at equidistant intervals of time. The free
form *soluta* is, on the contrary, characterized by the return of the
marked beats or ictus at unequal intervals of time; that is to say,
binary and ternary beats are freely mingled according to no rule
except that of satisfying the ear. This last form is, as we know, that
of the Gregorian melodies.[13]

"Free rhythm" means first of all — and this is its authentic meaning — that the succession of small measures in 2/8 or in 3/8 conform

[11] *Théorie du rythme*, p. 13.
[12] *Nombre Musical*, t. I, p. 9.
[13] *Nombre Musical*, t. II, pp. 2–4. See also pp. vi-vii.

no pre-established regular framework. The beats, instead of
eing regularly binary (a quarter-note) or regularly ternary (a
otted quarter-note), as is usually the case in our own music, fol-
w each other freely, mingling harmoniously. In other words, the
hythmic touching-points are not isochronous; they recur at un-
qual intervals of time, after two or after three time-units, accord-
ng to the choice of the composer. Free rhythm, as such, does of
ourse exclude triplets, which are absolutely prohibited. This is
ne of the happy consequences of the indivisibility of the primary
eat.

All notes retain their full value. The ternary beat is worth exactly
ne eighth-note more than the binary beat. Equality prevails, not
etween the compound beats, but between the primary beats or
mall units of which they are made up with their notes and
yllables.

And it is to a great extent this double principle of equality of sin-
le beats and inequality of compound beats that gives Gregorian
hythm its stateliness and nobility and a combination of steadiness
nd flexibility. Of *steadiness* because, as we have said, Gregorian
hythm is based on the indivisibility of the primary beat, just as the
odality of the chant is based on the diatonic scale, which might
lso be named the "indivisibility of the tone." Of *flexibility* by the
ree and harmonious combination of compound beats differing in
alue. Often, after a succession of binary beats there comes a ter-
ary beat which makes the melodic movement more supple and
ives it breadth just as it was in danger of taking on the character of
material and set measure. It is undoubtedly to this free succession
f the beats that some of the greatest charm of the Gregorian mel-
dy is due. We find a never-ending crosscurrent of movements,
nequal in duration, either binary or ternary, which, while re-
aining well defined, seem to remove even the suggestion of any-
hing mechanical. And it is indeed a delight to give oneself up to
his soothing of one's whole being which is so restful and peace-
iving, so well adapted too to the spiritual realities of which our
acred melodies sing. One could not dream of a more suitable in-
trument or one that would more adequately serve the high pur-
ose for which it had been created. This is the more true if we now
ealize that these compound beats do not rest on an "accent" but
n a light drop in the movement, regardless of volume of sound or
tress, and which is more often gentle and weak than strong. It is
lear that this lightness of the rhythmic touching-points also adds

greatly to the flexibility already given to the melody by the mix ture of binary and ternary elements.

c) The grouping of compound beats into larger units

It follows from all that has been said that compound beats ar related to the whole period which they help to build up throug the intermediary of groups, clauses and phrases. On this point bot ancient and modern theorists are in agreement, so we need nc dwell on it.

I will give one final quotation which sums up the teaching of a the authors; it is from M. Combarieu's *Théorie du Rythme dan la composition moderne d'après la doctrine antique* (p. 32, 37–39)

> Rhythm is made up of four elements which can be found i identical form:
> (1) in Greek and Latin lyrical poetry; (2) in the lyrical pc etry of modern languages, in which versification is still base on the accent in words; (3) in vocal and instrumental musi (of the classical period).
>
> These four elements are as follows: (a) the metrical foot; (b the clause, called in Greek *kolon*; (c) the period; (d) th strophe. But there is at the basis of rhythm an even smalle element than the metric foot to which we must draw attentio before beginning this analysis . . .; it is the primary beat.

Who will not recognize in the unanimous teaching of these au thors the very foundations of the Solesmes rhythmic theories an the various steps in the rhythmical synthesis which Dom Mocque reau has developed in his *Nombre Musical*?

3. COMPLETE INDEPENDENCE OF RHYTHM AND VOLUME OF SOUND OR STRESS

How are compound beats formed, or to be more exact, what i the rhythmic touching-point by which they are governed? Her we are approaching the crucial point of the whole synthesis c rhythm, the one over which so many quarrels have arisen. I refe to the very nature of rhythm. It is, moreover, the crucial point c the Solesmes Method. It is on this point that Dom Mocquerea most completely departed from the generally accepted teachin of all the schools, the one on which he most clearly showed himse

o be an innovator and, be it said, on which he truly renewed the
teaching of music. I shall have to keep to what is essential.

According to present-day theory, rhythm is a matter of volume
of sound created by a succession of strong (loud) beats and weak
(soft) beats. It is generally thus defined in textbooks on the theory
of music or on prosody. For most of our contemporaries this is a
first principle, beyond the realm of controversy and needing no
demonstration. I would add that even those who openly reject this
theory would be inclined to admit deep down in their subconscious
minds that the marked beat or first beat of a bar is a little louder
than the next one!

And yet, the whole of ancient poetry and all music, whether
ancient or modern, is in flagrant opposition to this theory of the
strong first beat. No musician worthy of the name would dream of
stressing every first beat in the bar when interpreting the great
works of our classical music. As for the poetical masterpieces of
antiquity, whether by Homer, Virgil, or Horace, with the law of
caesura, a law which is essential to the very make-up of verse, it is
impossible to contend that in them the beginning of a metrical foot
must be strong, since the caesura brings about the placing of final,
i.e., weak, syllables on the beginning of some metrical feet. This is
the great law of overlapping, hailed by both Maurice Emmanuel [14]
and by Dom Mocquereau,[15] which governs all prosody as well as
all rhythm. It is a hard fact which one cannot elude and for which
some valid explanation must be found. As a matter of interest I
refer the reader here to the rather strange controversy which took
place about forty years ago between two well-known masters of
meter, M. M. Bennett and Hendrickson, reported in the *American
Journal of Philology*, Vols. XIX and XX.[16]

Far more than either poetry or music, Gregorian art cannot be
reconciled with the theory of the strong beat. Right through the
Gregorian repertoire we find cases in which the tonic accent is
placed on one note only, whereas the final syllable, which is by
nature weak, or even the penultimate syllable of a dactylic word,
which is still less important, is laden with long notes or with neums
that in themselves bring about a drop in the movement and a

[14] "Grèce, Art gréco-roman," in *L'Encyclopédie de la Musique* (Paris,
1913) by Lavignac, t. I, pp. 471–472. Cf. P. Carraz, "L'accent et l'ictus dans
la métrique latine," *Rev. Grég.* (1951) pp. 45ff.; also, Dom Gajard, "L'ictus
et le rythme," *Rev. Grég.* (1921), pp. 212–223.

[15] *Nombre Musical*, t. II, pp. 294–301, 680–681, *et passim*.

[16] See *Nombre Musical*, t. II, pp. 674–681.

rhythmic touching-point. This is what I call the undeniable Gregorian fact, the very fact which, as I told you, at first scandalized the young Dom Mocquereau and made him turn away from Gregorian chant, which to him seemed in contradiction with the law of music.

If we find that the theory of the strong beat is in open contradiction with most poetical, musical and Gregorian compositions, this shows that it is, in itself, unacceptable as a theory.[17] We cannot agree with Mathis Lussy's statement when he naively writes at the very beginning of his *Traité de l'expression musicale*: "It is certain that the first beat of a bar must be strong. But it is surprising how seldom, in practice, this rule may be kept. One frequently comes across whole pages in which the first note of a bar is weak because it is the final one of a group or rhythm." And so we have to look for some other explanation. This is what Dom Mocquereau did and he succeeded in his quest.

He based his conclusions on a clear distinction which he made between the following: (a) the material or physical qualities of sound, i.e., pitch, volume and duration produced by a particular arrangement of the sound vibrations themselves (number, extent or duration); (b) the relationship thus forcibly created between the successive sounds, which could be high or low, loud or soft, short or long.

From this distinction Dom Mocquereau was led to conclude that rhythm cannot be identified with any one of the elements of pitch, volume, or duration. It consists in giving orderly construction to the movement created by variations in these three elements which are themselves of a material order. The perception of rhythm is chiefly an act of the mind and of a superior order. Its proper function is to make the relationship between these elements clear, and to grade them so that one and all may contribute to a unified whole, for without unity there can be no work of art. Rhythm is thus no longer an element which divides but one of *synthesis*, of grouping and fusion.

Rhythm is quite clearly an act of the mind, i.e., of an intellectual order, which takes hold of all the given elements, strips them of their own individual character and, with each one in its place, blends them in ever greater and more comprehensive units into the unity of a single movement. It is towards such unity that everything in rhythm imperiously tends.

[17] Cf. "L'ictus et le rythme," *Rev. Grég.* (1921). M. Emmanuel, *op. cit.*, pp. 470–476.

In other words, and according to the old definition, rhythm is "the art of beautiful movements," *ars bene movendi*, according to Saint Augustine, or, according to Plato, "order in movement."

Rhythm is therefore *a matter of movement* and is based on a relationship, not between weak and strong beats or vice-versa, but between *impetus* and *rest*. It consists essentially in an alternating rise and fall, lifting and replacing, in a series of undulations which may be compared to the undulating movement of waves. But the meeting-point of two waves has in itself nothing to do with volume of sound; it is, above all, the conclusion of one movement which constitutes the starting-point of the next. It is nothing more. This drop, this "rhythmical touching-point," the "rhythmical ictus," as we have called it, is therefore the end of a step, the putting down of the foot. This alighting or placing, which in itself is indifferent to strength or stress, will be strong or weak according to the Latin syllable which goes with it, or according to the part played by its note in the general layout of the musical phrase. The "strong beat" as such thus disappears; rhythm is no longer something material but becomes a thing of the mind. Such was the art of antiquity. I quote again from Maurice Emmanuel:

> The cultured art of the Greeks made something very alive of measure which was thereby the more free, and of which all the finer details could not be perceived by the ear alone. The mind had also to be used. . . . Here was something of an inward nature, of which the *spirit alone* could grasp the structure.[18]

I also truly mean *spirit*. This will be our keynote.

The intentional gentleness of the rhythmic touching-point affects the whole melodic line, giving it a wonderfully mellow, rounded and flexible quality. Instead of a series of loud percussions we get only one beautiful undulating line in which no material element comes to break the supple continuity.

Volume or strength, it should be noted, is not thereby lacking. Far from it. But instead of being periodically emphasized every two or three notes, it is merely a lovely shading spread over the whole phrase, giving it an even greater unity.

And so, not only the Gregorian melody but both musical and poetical rhythm have in one and the same time recovered their freedom. I should like here to refer to the professor who had given up trying to explain the poetical works of antiquity to his pupils,

[18] *Op. cit.*, pp. 471–474.

but who, when confronted with the theory which I have just given, wrote a long article to prove that Latin and Greek poets could only be read by the Method of Solesmes. I should also like to mention the case of a composer and teacher of composition in an American university who is also the author of a treatise on composition. He was perplexed on discovering the contradiction in terms between the theory of the strong beat and the musical works which he had to explain. He interrupted his teaching, asked for a vacation, came to England and then to France in order to find the key to the enigma, and found it only in the works of Dom Mocquereau. Here was the solution and an illuminating one of the supposedly insoluble problem.

4. INDEPENDENCE OF THE RHYTHMIC ICTUS AND THE LATIN TONIC ACCENT

We have now to consider the relationship between rhythm and the Latin word, a point which has given rise to so many discussions. After what has just been said on the nature of rhythm itself, lengthy explanations will be unnecessary. Moreover, only general principles will need to be agreed upon here; their application will be dealt with in the second part of this treatise.

The reason why the principle of necessary coincidence between rhythmic ictus and verbal accent has been taught so long is evident — it is the logical outcome of the theory of rhythm based on strength or stress. If the rhythmic ictus was strong, it had, obviously, to coincide with the tonic accent, which is the strong or stressed syllable in a word. Strength calls for strength. But if, as I have done, it can be shown that there is no "strong beat," that the rhythmic touching-point is in itself indifferently strong or weak, then there is no longer any need for the tonic accent to coincide with the ictus, which can adapt itself to any kind of syllable.

One can and should go even further. The rhythmic ictus being essentially a drop in a movement which has already begun and the end of an elementary rhythm, it follows that the syllable with which it has the greatest affinity is the final syllable of the word, and not the accented one. Clearly, the rhythmic touching-point, the drop or the end of a rhythm will be most in keeping with the drop or final syllable of the word. Ending calls for ending.

And if we consult all the Latin grammarians from the classical or even ante-classical era right down to the time when the Latin language disappeared and was changed into the romance languages, we find their testimony remarkably concordant. Dom Mocquereau has quoted and commented on them all and has written some forceful passages about them which I cannot even attempt to summarize.[19]

It follows, whatever we may think about it today, that the true characteristic of the Latin accent was not stress. This stress on the accent developed only very gradually, and, even so, it remained discreet in character. The accent, as the word itself indicates, belonged in the first place to the order of melody; it was a "tone," the melodic summit of the word, the converging point of all the syllables, the vital element, the soul of the word, *anima vocis*, as the ancient writers called it. Far from being a heavy material force or "thetic," it was an impetus, an *élan*, brief, light, vivid, swift and spiritual, "a point of light appearing spontaneously on the crest of a phrase," according to M. Laloy's happy expression.[20]

In other words, it occurred on the impetus of the verbal rhythm, on the arsis or "up-beat," as we would say today.[21] If you sing the Communion *Memento*, you will find everything in the right place; the undulating melodic and rhythmic line flows wonderfully freely. The words can be naturally sung and clearly pronounced because in each one there is a close relationship between rise and fall and between the accented and the final syllables, all of which constitutes the very essence of Latin accentuation. "There is no need," adds Dom Mocquereau, "to hammer out these accents in order to make them evident; on the contrary, from *high up* they radiate and shed their beams on the phrase as a whole. It is they and the varying ways in which they shed this light from the summit of rhythms which give the phrase movement, color and life. Hammer them out and all charm vanishes at once; the phrase becomes something material, heavy and earthbound."[22]

The whole repertory of the Golden Age of Plainsong bears witness to this. Except for reasons of phraseology, the accent is placed on the highest note of a word from which it radiates, and on the

---

[19] Cf. *Notions sur la rythmique grégorienne* (Tournai, 1944), pp. 51–60.

[20] *Revue musicale* (Dec., 1902).

[21] On this point Dom Mocquereau shows himself to be Dom Pothier's faithful disciple, as can be seen in his *Nombre Musical*, t. II, pp. 233–234, and especially pp. 613–624. He merely put on a solid foundation what Dom Pothier, who was embarrassed by his theory of rhythm based on stress, could see only intuitively and in outline, without any scientific proof of its legitimacy.

[22] *Nombre Musical*, t. II, p. 347.

impetus of the rhythm. This, of course, does not always happen; words must fulfill their function in the phrase, and the latter is always free to modify or change things according to its own needs. Nevertheless, the Gregorian composers have for the most part succeeded in allowing words to retain their native appearance with the accented syllable on the up-beat. And it is this which, in a great measure, gives the ancient melodies their freedom, flexibility, and lightness, their gentleness and captivating charm. (Communions *Memento verbi tui, Quinque prudentes virgines*; antiphons *Salve Regina, Ave Regina caelorum.*) I have no hesitation in adding that apart from this fundamental principle Plainsong is incomprehensible.

It is also one of the reasons why Plainsong may be looked upon as true music, because the element from which it was entirely formed and moulded both as regards rhythm and melody, i.e., the Latin accent, is first and foremost an element belonging to the order of music, and Plainsong is music. Truly a fairy godmother must have presided at the birth of the Gregorian melody!

It goes without saying that Gregorian art adds nothing to the reality of those philological and musical laws which existed before it and which govern all Greco-Roman poetry. But these laws had been forgotten and misrepresented for many centuries. It is Gregorian art which by its very existence has again revived the whole problem and at the same time provided the elements of a solution. For this it has earned the gratitude of musicians.

5. SUBORDINATION OF THE WORDS
TO THE MELODY

After all the preceding explanations, the essential point of the Solesmes Method, as stated in the above heading, need not be dwelled upon at length. It seems to follow naturally all that has hitherto been said and to which attention has already been drawn several times.

The principle itself is not open to doubt. "It was," says Dom Mocquereau, "recognized by all in ancient Greece and Rome." [23] And it is the outcome of the very nature of music, which was given by God to man that he might express the complex feelings which surge up in his heart and which poor human words, because they are too material and concrete, are unable to translate. I need only

[23] *Op. cit.*, II, 381.

remind you of Saint Augustine's magnificent commentary on the word *jubiláte* in his *Enarrationes super Psalmos* and the pleasure he takes in going back to it. If the function of music is to enhance the expressive power of words and even to go further, it becomes clear that it will be under no obligation to be perpetually moulded on them. The old adage so often quoted, *Musica non subjacet regulis Donati*, is particularly apt here.

Gregorian art is, in this connection, perhaps more characteristic than any other music. In no other, it would seem, does one find such liberties so deliberately taken with the words. And I am not only referring to the long vocalizations of a richness and splendor unknown elsewhere. A glance at any phrase in Gregorian chant will be convincing. With the exception of some hymns, entirely syllabic pieces are extremely rare. There is hardly a line without neums, which themselves distend syllables and thereby modify the normal shape of words. These modifications are of all kinds, melodic, quantitative, or rhythmical, and even affect volume. They all, of course, react on the rendering of a piece.

We cannot here enter into the practical application of this principle, as it would require endless development. Let it suffice for me to make definite statements on two points of a very different order: one concerning purely elementary rhythmical technique, which makes clear the position taken by us on this question and which completes what we have said about the independence of rhythm and the accent, the other on interpretation in general.

a) The rhythm of words and neumatic notation

Each of the two verbal forms, the spondee and the dactyl, if isolated, i.e., taken out of its context, has a clearly defined rhythm, as will be more fully explained in the second part of this treatise when we consider the Latin accent. In an elementary rhythm the spondee has an ictus on the final syllable; the accented syllable is on the up-beat of the elementary rhythm, whereas the dactyl has an ictus on the accented and on the final syllables of the elementary rhythm:

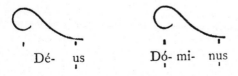

Dé- us   Dó- mi- nus

and the following is quite often to be met with in Gregorian pieces:

Ex. : *Gloria IX*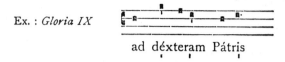

ad déxteram Pátris

But this form of rhythm in the isolated word may at any moment be modified either by the melody or by the neumatic grouping. When a neum occurs, for instance, on the accented syllable of a spondee or on the weak penultimate syllable of a dactyl, it automatically displaces the ictus and completely changes the normal rhythm of the word, as, for example, in the following excerpt from the Gloria of Mass II:

ad déxte-ram Pá-tris

In this group the normal rhythm of the words, which is already slightly modified in the spondee of *Pátris* by an ictus on the tonic accent, is completely changed in the dactyl *déxteram*, which loses the ictus both on the accented and the final syllables, and is given an ictus on its penultimate syllable, normally the weakest of all the syllables. Such cases occur very frequently in the Gregorian repertoire. Should we be shocked by this? Indeed not. And why not? Because the composer wished that it should be so, and he was perfectly free to make it so.

It should be quite clear that it is always the melodic form which takes precedence and, to avoid syncopation, this rule must be followed at the expense of the rhythm of the words. The principle of the subordination of the words to the music finds here one of its most important applications.

This law gives us no cause for complaint, for it is one of those that help to give Gregorian rhythm its independence and its flexibility. Inspiration would be very much hampered by its absence.

"Music," Dom Mocquereau tells us, "is too noble a lady; she knows that her resources are infinitely superior in number, variety, power and beauty to those of the merely spoken word. She reserves the right to use them as she pleases, not to the detriment of the words but to their advantage. She explains their meaning, enhances their expression and conveys their lessons to the very depth of the human soul."

He adds later, after he has vindicated the rights of the melody: "Nevertheless, it must also be stated that these rights never degenerate into capricious or blind tyranny, indiscriminately exercised over all the parts of the musical period. On the contrary, no chant better than the Roman treats words with such consideration and deference. Very often, as we have proved, it adapts its movements to those of the words, it moulds its rhythms and intonations on them and keeps to their material form throughout whole phrases and periods.

When the melody frees itself it seems almost always to do so with some regret. It takes the greatest care, uses ingenious devices and tactful consideration in order to allow the companion words to retain some of their influence. If, however, the limitations of the words impose too many restrictions on the melody, and the latter is unable to interpret the words according to their meaning in its own way and to decorate them with suitable melisma, then the melody at once proclaims its rights. But even when the melody asserts itself most rigorously, it nevertheless takes infinite pains to preserve the linking of syllables, thus maintaining the unity of the words, of which it gently stretches the parts without ever separating or breaking them." [24]

b) Words, melody and interpretation

My next point, which is of a very different nature, has been suggested by remarks often made to us. This law of subordination of the words to the melody obviously applies only to the actual technique of rhythm, to what I have described elsewhere, perhaps not very aptly, as its "mechanism," a word which is easily understood. *It applies in no way to the inner meaning of the compositions themselves.* We have sometimes been accused of teaching that no notice need be taken of the words and that the melodies should be interpreted as if they were pure music without any words! This clearly is a completely mistaken view.

This rhythmic "mechanism" (grouping into compound beats, composite rhythms, etc.), which depends on the form of the words and still more on the melody which accompanies them (neums, timbre, etc.), is a very different thing from the composer's mental image concealed under these signs, or rather, which he has tried

[24] *Nombre Musical*, t. II, p. 282, 394.

to translate by these signs and which the interpreter has again to discover. Undoubtedly, the shape of the melodic line, the intervals, the general modal character or modulations of parts, the accents and the fluctuations of the rhythm, whether composite or simple, as well as the marks of expression in the manuscripts — all these are elements of the highest value which must on no account be neglected. Yet, all this can never eclipse the actual *meaning* of the words themselves, which takes first place if it be true that Gregorian chant is above all a liturgical text clothed in a melody which is destined to be a commentary, an explanation, and to set forth the value of the words. It is therefore the words that must first be looked into. Any other procedure would result in a purely subjective rendering and would consequently be without value, since it is the meaning of the whole work which has to be discovered and expressed in its interpretation. We cannot speak too categorically on this point.

To put it briefly, the rhythmic "mechanism" depends, especially in ornate chants, on the neumatic grouping and, in syllabic chant, on verbal forms; the general interpretation (expression, speed, special character) comes above all from the meaning of the words.

And yet, although we withdraw nothing from what has just been said, we must add that it would be equally mistaken to look only at the words when interpreting a piece of Gregorian chant and to ignore the requirements of the melody or its musical aspect. This musical aspect is precious if we are to enter into the Church's intention in choosing a particular passage for a particular circumstance. The same passage may be given several acceptable interpretations. Only the melody's clear commentary on the words will tell us which to select. Thus, words and melody throw light upon one another, and the combined study of both is the basis of any sincere and authentic interpretation of "the sung prayer of the Church," which is Plainsong.

6. TRADITIONAL MARKS OF EXPRESSION

I come now to my last point, relating to another aspect of this subject which differs very much from what has already been considered, but which must be mentioned as it is one of the most characteristic of the Solesmes Method.

The Solesmes editions can be recognized by the addition of signs to the notation as printed in the Vatican edition. There are three of these: the *dot* doubles the length of the note it follows and most often marks a small cadence; the *vertical episema* under a note marks small rhythmical subdivisions; the *horizontal episema* above a note adds an expression mark. I will confine myself to expressive marks as indicated chiefly by the horizontal episema. Where do they come from?

They come from a tradition which was preserved in the oldest manuscripts and which showed, down to the smallest detail, how to interpret the chant.[25] This was a universal tradition and was identical in all the countries of the West. It was a very early tradition which in all probability came from Rome and goes back to the time of St. Gregory. If honest recognition of scientific and historical facts compels us to accept this tradition, its artistic interest and still more its religious significance make this a duty, so much do these marks of expression enhance the power and the spirit of prayer of the liturgical melodies.

I should, at this juncture, go back to the work on paleography which has been carried on at Solesmes for the last century and for which Dom Mocquereau was chiefly responsible. As I have already said, it was Dom Mocquereau's paleographical studies which spurred him on to his work on rhythm. But this is a world in itself. It will suffice to remind the reader that it was to Solesmes in the first place that the task of drawing up the Vatican edition had been given. In preparation for this a large number of photographs of manuscripts from many countries and periods had been collected, and they formed quite a library at the Abbey. There were about six hundred complete manuscripts as well as a countless number of fragments.

In order to restore the melodies of these ancient pieces, it was necessary to collate them into great synoptic charts. Soon it was noticed that a number of the oldest and best manuscripts — those which, according to the wishes of Pius X, were to serve as a basis for the restored melodies — had a number of additional signs which were not to be found in the other manuscripts. Besides the usual neumatic notation, there were a number of marks of expression shown by letters or signs or changes in the shape of the neums. Patient and careful comparative study of the charts made it possible to discover the meaning of most of these signs, first of all those in the manuscripts of St. Gall.

[25] Cf. "La tradition rythmique dans les manuscrits," *Rev. Grég.* (1923), pp. 121–132; 153–167; reproduced in *Monographie IV*.

But what is the value of these indications? Were they personal to this or that monk of St. Gall, and did he, on his own initiative, add them as an afterthought? Or do they represent a tradition, and if so, what tradition?

To put it briefly, a critical study of the oldest Sangallian manuscripts, those which we call "rhythmical," reveals the most complete agreement between them all. Piece by piece, neum by neum, down to the smallest detail in the entire and immense liturgical repertoire (there are hundreds of pieces) we find agreement so complete that it can only be explained if looked upon as the faithful recording of a pre-existing traditional interpretation.

Moreover, the manuscripts of St. Gall are not the only ones that give these indications. Their equivalent may be found in all the schools, but there are three particular schools in which the testimony is just as clear and precise; these are the schools of Metz, Chartres and Nonantalia. Curiously enough, each of these three schools has its own particular system of writing, and each one differs from the other as much in the manner of writing neums as in that of indicating marks of expression, which facts go to prove their complete mutual independence. Such unanimity between all the schools can only be explained by their faithful adherence to a common source whose tradition had been religiously preserved. Obviously this common source must have been the same both for rhythm and melody. Consequently, if the melodic tradition comes from Rome, the rhythmic tradition also comes from Rome and, as such, is Roman and of early origin.

This was a universal tradition, a Roman tradition, and a very early tradition. Everything in it commands our acceptance — scientific facts, historical facts, artistic interest. But there is more to it. Have you ever been struck by the immense strength of will which our forefathers of the Middle Ages must have exerted to preserve this early tradition so completely unimpaired during several centuries, in spite of differences in temperament, customs and taste, and for something of such seemingly secondary importance as a chant? This is a fact which, I think, opens up wide horizons. Such determination shows us first the importance which was attached to sung prayer, but more especially the prevailing sense of the Church as a corporate body. For these men of profound faith, it was not simply a matter of any kind of prayer, even artistically expressed; it meant the liturgical, social, and catholic prayer, the prayer of the Church. The Church had a chant of her own, or better still, she had her own interpretation, and no individual felt that he was qualified to substitute his own for that of the Church.

I cannot help finding in such unanimity between the churches of the Middle Ages in keeping to the Roman interpretation of the chant one of the most beautiful tributes ever paid to the unity and catholicity of the Church. In apologetics it could be used as a sound argument, although it may not often have been seen in this light. For my part, I shall never forget an Episcopalian bishop, a visitor from America, who, in the presence of such extraordinary unanimity which, humanly speaking, is inexplicable, broke down and asked to be instructed in the Catholic religion.

God knows how much more life comes back to these beloved melodies, how much warmer, more moving and even more spiritual they become when they find their true interpretation and expression. Once again, this is not merely a question of artistic interest; it is one of prayer, of the *solemn, official prayer of the Church*. Moreover, the Church, the Spouse of Christ, extending throughout space, is equally independent of time and human vicissitudes. We have nothing to lose if, like little children, we too ask to be taught by her. Is this not once again for us a way of being truly "Catholic"?

Jesus Christ yesterday, today, and forever!

Elements Constituting the Synthesis

Such, in brief, are the main points of the rhythmical synthesis put forward by Dom Mocquereau in his *Nombre Musical Grégorien*. The slight and very imperfect summary which I have attempted to give will at least suffice to show its perfect coherence, unity and simplicity.

In it, Gregorian rhythm is shown to be in the first place musical. It takes into account the rights of the verbal text to which it belongs. Yet, due respect is paid to the melody, and precedence is always given to the latter. Moreover, the recognized part played by the accent singularly reduces conflicts and wonderfully contributes to this synthesis. In rhythm, as so understood, there is nothing rigid or mechanical. We have only one beautiful line whose purity and infinite flexibility cannot be altered.

The accent? This is a rise in the melody, something strong yet gentle, a spiritual *élan*, an element of coordination, or, better still, the principle of the unity of the word.

The word? This is a melody in itself, a rhythm which is well defined, complete and perfect, autonomous, but which can, if need be, give way to the melody and the phrase. It never stands in the way of the musical rhythm, since there is complete subordination of the word to the melody, and of the word to the group, which is a unit of greater importance.

Volume or stress? This is no longer materially heavy, crushing the rhythm, weighing it down and making it halt, but one of the great factors of cohesion and unity. "Volume is above measure, belongs entirely to rhythm as a whole and to the greater rhythm, which has no need of its assistance in organizing the details of its movements. By progressive crescendos and decrescendos from note to note and from group to group it links them together and fuses them into one organic whole. It is thus the sap and very life-blood of rhythm."[26]

Duration? Melody? These, like stress, contribute to the rhythmic synthesis, and even more so, since everything finally depends upon them.

And, last of all, rhythm? Here we have the royal, the supreme element, one belonging to the highest order, of a scarcely material nature, dominating all other elements, moving freely among them and of its own virtue bringing about the unification of them all. It is free from any angularity in its movement, from any set time or pre-established grouping, infinitely flexible yet remarkably definite, since all sounds and syllables, instead of wandering at random, find in it an exact and well-defined place. Finally, it gives us a broad and harmonious redistribution of time in which all the constituent elements, far from being in conflict with one another, complete each other. Rhythm clothes them, and in a way spiritualizes them and gives them movement, beauty, and life. It is thus truly the art of beautiful movements, *ars bene movendi*.

I do not deny that along with this wonderful flexibility there is the disciplinary side to the rendering of the chant. Singers have not only to follow purely technical rules but must also conform to the traditional interpretation of the chant as preserved in the old manuscripts. This gives to their singing an impersonal, detached and austere character. It would be very much simpler if they could follow the dictates of their own temperament or fancy!

But let us turn again to one of Camille Bellaigue's apt expressions when, in speaking of this assuredly severe discipline, he

[26] *Nombre Musical*, t. I, p. 62.

says: "Who will not see how much of weakness and flabbiness it keeps out of the chant, and how much it thus gains in masculine vigor and beauty?" [27]

And is it not true that such are the conditions under which all religious art is produced? I should like to complete this first part of my statement by the following considerations taken from Abbé Georges Duret's "Théorie de l'art chrétien," published in the beautiful volume of *Tailles directes d'Henri Charlier*.[28]

> Christian technique may be recognized by a certain degree of austerity. "*Ab exterioribus ad interiora.*" It avoids ornamentation, agitation, distractions; indolence is repugnant to it and it has a horror of morbid pleasures. In order to handle with purity what is material and carnal, it has a direct method by which it reaches what is essential in each object. There is a certain poverty in its grandeur. Hence the need for periodical reform in Christian art just as in all other art.

> But if a secret spirit thus draws art inwards, it is only that it may be directed to the heights. "*Ab interioribus ad superiora.*" Christian art may be recognized by its spiritual radiance. If austere, it is not melancholy, but illuminated by aesthetic grace, symbol of true grace. Even when depicting struggle and suffering, it remains serene and intimately and cordially peaceful. A mystical impulse urges the soul on from moral to theological virtues, from duty to charity and to a blossoming of spirituality.

> These conditions apply, no doubt, to all true art, and every period of great and balanced achievements has seen them at least partially realized. But it remains true that a Christian who practices his faith in Christian surroundings is more quickly aware of and far more deeply sensitive to any disorder than a pagan or a heretic would be and has better means for applying a remedy. It is also true that religion sets before the artist a higher ideal, indeed one that is unique. Thus in safeguarding Christian art, the Church safeguards all art.

These lines, it is true, were written about statuary and not about music, but do they not perfectly well apply to Gregorian art, which is perhaps the most alive and most spiritual of all religious art?

[27] "Le Chant Grégorien," in the *Revue des Deux-Mondes* (1898), p. 368. Reproduced in *Les Époques de la Musique*, p. 100.
[28] *Les Tailles directes d'Henri Charlier* (Wépion, Belgium: Librairie du Mont-Vierge, 1927), pp. 33–34.

PART II

PRACTICAL RULES OF
INTERPRETATION

We have now given in broad outline both the rhythmical theories of Solesmes and the general principles which, we think, should regulate the interpretation of Plainsong. Let us now descend from theory to practice and set forth the practical rules for interpretation which are the outcome of these theories.[1] Obviously, to be complete I should have to dwell at some length on several of them, but I shall confine myself to what is essential: to an enumeration of the rules, with a few brief explanations and some examples.

These rules can be divided into two quite distinct categories: those which concern rhythmical technique as such and those relating to style. The former more especially constitute the Method of Solesmes, although the latter also form part of it and may be looked upon as very nearly as important.[2]

[1] In order to fully understand all these rules a good knowledge of the working of the rhythmic synthesis, of the functioning of the various parts of what I would call its mechanism is necessary: the formation of an elementary rhythm, a compound beat, a composite rhythm, etc. For this I refer the reader to the various treatises and methods on the subject: *Nombre Musical Grégorien* by Dom Mocquereau; *Précis de Rythmique* by M. Le Guennant; and to my *Notions sur la Rythmique Grégorienne*. Here I shall keep to purely practical rules of interpretation.

[2] To illustrate these rules, there are two sets of recordings: the first made in 1930 by His Master's Voice, the second during the summer of 1951 by Decca. In spite of some slight defects, taken as a whole these records do, we think, give a fairly accurate idea of the rhythm and style of Plainsong as interpreted by Solesmes.

A. Rules of Rhythmical Technique

1. RESPECT FOR THE PRIMARY BEAT

We consider the indivisibility of the primary beat as a basis of utmost importance, i.e., it is impossible to split up this primary beat into smaller units, as is the custom in our own contemporary music. If the value of the primary beat is, for instance, an eighth-note, there will be no sixteenth or thirty-second notes. This means that each note (or each syllable, more especially in a dactyl) must be given its full time-value and no fraction of it sacrificed. Thus, for practical purposes, all have the same time-value. Anything that would tend to diminish this value, e.g., triplets, quadruplets, must be strictly avoided. This applies in every case, even to neums occurring on the weak penultimate syllable of a dactyl, and, in syllabic chant, to penultimate syllables themselves and to the accented syllables of dactyls.

The application of this fundamental principle is unfortunately often overlooked, with the result that we inevitably get a negation and travesty of Gregorian art and of what I would call its spirit. If, on the contrary, it is scrupulously applied, the dignity and beauty of the melody are greatly enhanced.

Here in great measure lies the secret of the firmness and impersonal character of the chant, its profound serenity and remarkable purity of line. Sing, for instance, *Kyrie XI* both ways: with sixteenth-notes on the syllable -*ri*, shooting down onto the two climacus on *e*, or, on the contrary, with scrupulous care, giving each note its full time-value. You will then understand what I mean. Try the same with the hymn *Vexilla Regis*.

The following should, however, be kept in mind: (a) this equality is one of duration and, as such, does not affect the melody or apply to stress; so there is no fear of monotonous uniformity or lifelessness. (b) This equality in time-values is tempered by the action of the rhythm which informs and transforms every unit so that here again there is no risk of any material rigidity. (c) Since we speak of music, this equality in time-value can only be *relative* and never mathematically or metronomically absolute. All these points will be made clear in the following pages.

I may here be allowed to say that although this principle of the indivisibility of the primary beat is easy to understand and readily acceptable, its practical realization seems to be extremely difficult judging by what one hears almost everywhere. There is, to my mind, only one way by which it can be achieved, and that is to analyze the melody by compound beats. I shall return to this shortly.

2. EXACT TIME-VALUE OF THE COMPOUND BINARY AND TERNARY BEATS

This is the logical outcome of our first rule. With elementary rhythms acting as an intermediary, these primary beats link themselves together to form compound binary and ternary beats, thus clearly marking off each step of the rhythmic movement.

Since primary beats are indivisible and of equal duration, it follows as a happy consequence that a ternary beat lasts (I think all mathematicians will agree with me) exactly one beat longer than a compound binary beat, and it is from this that the freedom of Gregorian rhythm is partly derived.

We have here one of the most important aspects of Gregorian interpretation, one to which attention cannot be too frequently drawn. A triplet, by reducing three single beats to the value of two single beats, i.e., that of a compound binary beat, undermines at its base the very idea of freely measured rhythm and makes it regularly measured.

It is from the double principle of equality of single beats and inequality of compound beats that the melodic line of Plainsong derives so much dignity and nobility. The chant thus becomes a product of well-defined values, of firmness and flexibility, soothing to the soul and inclining it to contemplation. To illustrate this, sing, for instance, the Communion *Memento verbi tui* of the twentieth Sunday after Pentecost with its rocking and suggestive lilt, or the last *Kyrie IV*, or the *Benedictus* of Mass IX.

We beg all those who wish Plainsong to be true to itself not to fail in maintaining its clarity, its bearing, I might say, its perfect distinction. Only thus will it be possible for it to fulfill its blessed function of sanctifying souls by bringing them peace and recollection.

It is, however, important that this small complex unit, the compound beat, should keep its true character and that both its internal economy and organic unity should be respected.

a) Its organic unity

This can be achieved if the single beats of which it is made up, more especially in ornate chant, are so blended as to form a perfect legato. The note with the ictus is the most important note, the essential one (I do not say the loudest), it is the only one on which, for practical purposes, the movement of the rhythm rests. The second note in a binary compound beat and the two last notes in a ternary compound beat are the outcome of this first beat and are merely its complement, its overflow and shadow. They must not therefore be detached from it, nor must they be emphasized or weakened, and, above all, they must not be lengthened at the expense of the first note. They should be treated lightly so as to be united with it and, as it were, prolong it, while they themselves keep their full time-value and even their own degree of strength. They differ from the ictic note only by their rhythmical function, and this in itself will be a first step toward softening any possible rigidity in the equality of primary beats, without adversely affecting the complete unity of the compound beat. If this rule is kept, it will give the chant a grandeur and style which cannot be obtained in any other way.

It is almost exclusively in syllabic chant, and principally when the accent is on the up-beat, i.e., when the tonic accent comes on the *last* single beat of a compound beat, that this last single beat is less closely linked to the one or two preceding beats (as will be explained later). Meanwhile it remains enclosed within the unity of a single rhythmic movement.

Moreover, the ictus and the compound beat which it governs are so closely united that, later on, where we speak of the synthesis of a composite rhythm, the terms "arsic compound beat" and "arsic ictus" will be interchangeable.

b) Its internal economy or value

This will be achieved if it is centered exactly on the rhythmic ictus (or drop in the elementary rhythm) which affects the compound beat, and if it is given its true time-value, whether binary or ternary, as the case may be. There need be no fear of this making the chant sound material or mechanical; the contrary is the case. Flexibility is only possible where all is exact, when every element is in its right place.[3]

[3] I need only remind my readers of how to decide which will be the ictic note on which the compound beat rests. Three rules suffice, at least in our

It is only on condition of being thus constituted as distinct and organic entities that compound beats can be incorporated into the greater rhythm, of which they are the necessary basis.

I have already spoken of the difficulty experienced by singers in maintaining well-defined time-values, i.e., equality in the time-value of the primary beat and also the exact value of compound beats. The two are closely connected and inseparable. The lack of well-defined time-values and slackness in keeping to them have greatly contributed to bringing the chant into disrepute, especially among musicians. I should like here to suggest a practical way out of the difficulty. This is to make singers analyze a Gregorian melody by compound beats, counting 1-2, 1-2-3 as required. This should be done systematically and frequently until the singers can change with ease from a binary to a ternary compound beat or measure and vice versa.

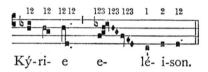

This exercise may seem childish to the reader, but it is not an easy one. Moreover, it never fails to give good results, especially if care is taken to mark the beginning of each compound beat with some slight but clear movement of the hand or finger. To my mind, this practice is necessary and the *sine qua non* condition for training a schola. It is also the only sure way of correcting irregularity in speed in a piece which is already known. I attribute the great progress made in France during the last years to this practice of counting. Many choirmasters have realized its necessity and have made it the basis of their teaching. The scholas which have not been willing to accept the discipline of this training can be recognized at once.

Solesmes editions. In ornate chant the following will have an ictus: notes marked with a *vertical episema*; all *lengthened notes* (dotted notes, notes preceding the quilisma); the *first note of each neum*, unless this is immediately preceded or followed by an ictic note. To this may be added that in syllabic chants, except for recognized formulae, the ictus should be given preferably to *final syllables* of words and to the *accented syllable in dactyls*. I say "preferably" because many other elements may intervene, such as the melodic line, etc. *See Nombre Musical*, t. II, ch. VIII, IX, X.

3. GENTLE DESCENTS

This too is a very important point and is as essential to the right interpretation of the chant as is the accuracy of its rhythm. We have already seen that the ictus or touching-points of the rhythm have in themselves no direct connection with volume of sound or stress, and that it would be a gross error to look upon them as "strong beats." This, in spite of outdated theories, applies to all music and is particularly true of Plainsong, for Plainsong is by definition Latin and based on the Latin word, where all final syllables are light and free from stress.

This does not mean that the ictus is never strong; it can be so when, for example, it coincides with an accented syllable or because of its position in the melodic line. But this happens *per accidens*, because of some clause outside itself. Of itself the ictus has no connection with stress.

Now is the time to quote once again these lines which do such honor to Dom Mocquereau's artistic sense. He is speaking of the "varying shades of expression" which may be given to ictic notes in the center of groups, but what he says is equally true of all ictic notes:

a) Sometimes the ear is made aware of the rhythmic subdivisions by the gentle and discreet emphasis which marks the ictic note.

b) At other times the legato is smoother and more intimate; the rhythmic subdivisions are as if veiled and can hardly be detected.

c) Still more often, whether the passage in question be slow or rapid, these secondary subdivisions disappear entirely and blend into an uninterrupted legato, leaving one with only a sense of the broad and full undulation of the musical phrase. The touching-point is then so soft and caressing that it remains imponderable, more spiritual than material; only our interior senses can take cognizance of it if they will, and this, moreover, is unnecessary.[4]

As a matter of fact, in the Gregorian melodies the ictus is in most cases very gentle. This partly explains why the melodies are so spiritual and immaterial in character, so pacifying and so liberating, impregnated as they are with the great spirituality of Ca-

[4] *Nombre Musical*, t. I, p. 417.

tholicism and with the sanctity of the monks who conceived them.

Most of us have been brought up on the theory of the "strong beat," or rather, since this habit was neither conscious nor reasoned, it has become for us second nature. Reaction against this tendency will therefore be most necessary, first in our elementary exercises and then in our singing. Consequently, if, as we have suggested, Gregorian pieces are analyzed by compound beats of two and three beats, and a gesture is used to mark each of the ictic notes, it will be necessary to avoid with care any hammering out of the notes as this would inevitably emphasize the ictus and make it louder. The relationship of voice to gesture is obvious, given the unity of man's make-up, and, whatever is indicated in the gesture will be faithfully reproduced by the voice. A harsh, angular, material beat will produce harsh, material and soulless singing. In marking the ictus with the finger, great care must therefore be taken to do this as gently and as discreetly as possible. The movement should be merely a touching, designed to show plastically the reality of the rhythmical fall.

4. THE LATIN TONIC ACCENT

I shall not again return to the principle which governs the accent. It is well known; one has only to refer to the Latin grammarians and to the poetical works of the ancient classics to learn that the true Latin tonic accent is by nature light and arsic. To express this more clearly it should be stated that its normal place is *on the arsis of the elementary rhythm, on the up-beat in spondaic words;*[5] *on the arsis of the composite rhythm, although on the ictus in dactylic words.*

It follows from this that the accent is always in a more suitable place when it is on the arsis of the musical rhythm. And it will be found to be so treated in the Gregorian melodies where, even when it is ictic, it usually remains on the arsis of the composite rhythm.

Naturally, the composer, who is by definition a creator, is perfectly free to follow his genius and his inspiration. He may, therefore, if he chooses to do so, change the normal aspect of words and

[5] These two words *spondee* and *dactyl* which I have chosen in preference to the technical expressions paroxytone and proparoxytone are used here not in their prosodic sense (long and short) but in their accentual acceptation (accented and unaccented syllables). The spondee (paroxytone) has the accent on the penultimate syllable: *Déus*; and the dactyl (proparoxytone) has the accent on the antepenultimate syllable: *Dóminus*.

even completely ignore the accent in favor of the general musical line. In such a case the singer can only interpret the text as it has been given to him and to the best of his ability. It is, however, a fact that, in most cases, composers have discovered the secret of combining perfection of musical line with respect for the Latin idiom.

a) The accent on the up-beat

If the accent is on the up-beat, on the arsis of the elementary rhythm, or to put it more clearly, on the second beat of a binary compound beat or on the third beat of a ternary compound beat, it remains indissolubly linked with the following syllable towards which it irresistibly tends with gentle and spiritual energy. Thus are safeguarded both the unity and life of the word, *anima vocis*, the ancient writers called it. And so I beg of you, singers, to allow the accent to keep its native lightness at all costs. Do not hammer it out, do not make of it something material or heavy; launch it and give it its full scope. To achieve this, any heavy or incisive stress must be avoided. Lighten the accent, soften it, round it off, broaden it a little. Let it hover, so to speak, before the melody alights on the last syllable of the word. It must be discreet, supple, soft, immaterial, "a luminous point which readily appears on the crest of phrases," as M. Laloy has said. Such is the Latin accent which has fashioned both the melody and the rhythm of our Gregorian melodies.

Look, for instance, at the group *Scit enim Páter véster* from the antiphon *Nolite solliciti esse*; or the group *fundátus enim erat* from the antiphon *Iste sanctus* for a martyr; or the beginning of the Communion for the twentieth Sunday after Pentecost, *Meménto verbi tui*, etc; the group *in vasis suis cum lampádibus* of the Communion for virgins, *Quinque prudentes virgines*; the group *Hódie in Jordáne* from the antiphon for Epiphany, *Hodie*, etc. Examples are to be found throughout the entire Gregorian repertoire.

b) The accent on the down-beat

Should the accent occur on the down-beat, i.e., on the ictus, either in syllabic chant or ornate chant, this will not make its rendering any easier but just the contrary. The accent on the down-beat no longer has the flexible freedom of the accent on the upbeat and is necessarily a little heavier, tending to become more material.

This tendency must be firmly resisted and the accent lightened and made to form part of the greater rhythm.

Composers of the golden age of Plainsong possessed in an eminent degree an understanding of the Latin genius. In their beautiful compositions the tonic accent, even when it falls on the ictus or on the down-beat of an elementary rhythm, remains melodically on the arsis of the composite rhythm. Take, for example, *Kyrie XI*, the Introit *Exsurge* for Sexagesima, the Introit *Salve Sancta Parens* of Our Lady, etc. I could quote numerous examples on every page of our chant books.

Even on final cadences, where it is nearly always embodied in the final thesis of the phrase, the accent keeps something of its arsic character, in both simple and ornate cadences:

Here it is still tending towards the final note. This is an important point. It is because most choirs neglect it that we so often hear heavy and lifeless phrase-endings.

We must also remember that the true and essential nature of Latin accentuation does not lie in stress, which was added later as a corollary, but it is to be found in the relationship of impetus to fall between the accented and the final syllable. Whether in reading or singing, every time you have made this relationship between the accent and the final syllable of the word felt, your accentuation has been perfectly sound, even if you have hardly stressed the accented syllable. If, on the contrary, you have not made this relationship of rise and fall felt, your accentuation has been faulty or non-existent, however much you may have stressed the accented syllable. In fact, the more you stress and materialize this accented syllable, the more you isolate it from other syllables, and, in consequence, the more you destroy the supreme aim of accentuation, which is to preserve the unity of the word.

c) The accent is ignored by the melody

Finally, there are cases where the composer has, in some words, obviously ignored the tonic accent, having in mind only the musical line. He has a perfect right to do this. One does not compose in order to set every word to music, but in order to translate into music a single idea expressed in a number of words. In such a case each element is a part of the whole and must take its own place in that whole, e.g., the word *coeli* in the *Sanctus* of Mass IX; the word *Dómini* in the *Benedictus* of Mass XI, etc.

The melodic line should here be given first place, according to the old saying: *Musica non subjacet regulis Donati*. Moreover, the word will be sufficiently protected if the final syllable is no stronger than the one which normally carries the accent.

THE RESPECT DUE TO SPONDAIC AND DACTYLIC VERBAL FORMS

Before we leave the question of the tonic accent, let us return for a moment to the distinguishing features of spondaic and dactylic verbal forms in order to clarify certain points.

In speaking earlier of the Latin tonic accent, we made a distinction between two verbal forms: the *spondaic* form, in which the tonic accent is on the up-beat of the elementary rhythm:

De - us

the *dactylic* form, in which the accent is on the down-beat of the elementary rhythm, but on the arsis of the composite rhythm: [6]

Do- mi-nus

[6] I purposely refrain from going into what distinguishes an elementary rhythm from a composite rhythm. I only wish to show how, in an elementary rhythm, the accented syllable of a dactyl is merely ictic whereas, in a composite rhythm, the arsic value of the Latin accent will normally give an arsic character to the ictus itself.

In syllabic chant, except in cases where melody and rhythm indicate the contrary, it is important that each of these two forms should keep its own rhythmic features and particularly at cadences, especially in psalmody. I draw your attention here to a few special cases.

a) The rhythm of the dactylic accent

Many people, in their zeal for making the accent come on the up-beat, upset the balance of dactylic cadences by putting, for example, an ictus on the syllable which precedes the accent:

qui timet Dóminum
ı   ı

with the result that most often both the accented syllable and the penultimate syllable (*Dó-mi*) become two sixteenth-notes.

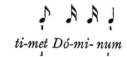

ti-met Dó-mi- num
ı   ı

We thus get a limping, fictitious rhythm which goes against the indivisibility of the primary beat and destroys the quiet flow of the melody.

We should not forget that "the accent on the up-beat" is not an aim in itself but a means to an end. In the normal rhythm of a word it occurs in spondaic words only, in which its chief function is to give rhythm to the word, i.e., by placing the final syllable on the ictic drop or fall and thus to mark the close connection between them. All this applies more or less also to a dactylic rhythm, in which the impetus of the accent is safeguarded by the arsic character of the ictus which bears it, and where its relationship to what follows is obvious. There is, however, this difference: in a spondee we have a relationship within an elementary rhythm, and in a dactyl a relationship within a composite rhythm.

Do not hesitate, therefore, in dactylic cadences, to put an ictus under the accent of the dactyl:

qui timet Dóminum
ı   ı   ı

as this will allow the three syllables to keep their normal time-value and to be pronounced at a quiet, natural and harmonious pace. It will, in fact, allow them to maintain their own obvious rhythm.

b) The duration of the dactylic accent

Our old cantors used to lengthen the accented syllable at the expense of the weak penultimate syllable. A desire to react against this practice has given rise to another very common fault. This consists in unduly shortening the accented syllable and giving too much importance to the penultimate syllable, which thereby becomes accented. All things considered, this fault comes from the same cause as the preceding one, that is, from imposing a false rhythm on the dactyl. If the ictus were clearly placed on the accent and on the final syllable, order would at once be restored.

We must, however, realize that the equality in value of the three syllables of a dactyl is merely theoretical. In fact, even if the three syllables are given exactly the same time-value, the small penultimate syllable, squeezed as it is between two ictic syllables, of which one is accented, cannot but be slightly effaced. This is only a logical consequence of the nature of rhythm which inevitably makes ictic notes preponderant. The resulting relative effacement of the penultimate in no way implies a shortening of its time-value.

c) The final monosyllable

It should now be clear that a final monosyllable loses its accent and, when it comes after a spondee, forms a dactyl with the latter. This is especially the case when the final monosyllable is grammatically united to the spondee, as, for instance, in the passive forms of verbs: *fáctus est = Dóminus*. Even when it keeps its logical importance, e.g., *laudámus te, glorificámus te*, etc., it should never be treated with harsh, material emphasis. In accordance with what we recommended for the Latin accent in general, it should be led up to and pronounced gently.

5. THE COMPOSITE RHYTHM

After this semi-digression on gentle endings and on the *élan* of the Latin accent, we must again take up our study of the synthesis of rhythm.

Once their limits and constitution as units have been clearly defined, compound beats do not remain in juxtaposition. Because they end on the up-beat they require a sequel and are, therefore, not conclusive. They are essentially sociable and intended to be grouped together and to enter into relationship with one another. They, in their turn, thus form units of a higher order, comparable in every way (although on a larger scale) with the smaller units with which we have so far been dealing.

In other words, just as single beats are grouped together in the relationship of rise and fall to form elementary rhythms, so compound beats, acting as units and carried forward by their governing ictus, group themselves together in the relationship of rise and fall so as to form composite rhythms. Some (arsic) launch the movement; others (thetic) gradually hold it back or even bring it to either provisional or final rest.

Here for instance are three *Sanctus*: (a) Sanctus VII; (b) Sanctus XII; (c) Sanctus XVII.

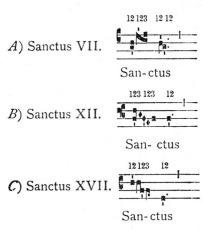

A) Sanctus VII.

San-ctus

B) Sanctus XII.

San- ctus

C) Sanctus XVII.

San-ctus

In (a) there are four compound beats. The first two on *so-lah* and on *doh'-ti-doh'* obviously show a rise or impetus in the melody. The last two are on the dotted (doubled) notes of the clivis, each of which is a binary compound beat; these show the resulting fall in the melody. We have here two arses and two theses.

In (b) there are only three compound beats; all three rest on the ictic note, *ray*. But in the first, a rising interval of a third gives a slight impetus or *élan* to this small portion of melody, whereas in the second a complete melodic descent acts as a brake on the movement and prepares the final resting-point on the third. We have here one arsis and two theses.

In (c) there are also three compound beats. The first starts in full swing at the top of the melody; the second in its descent also prepares the third, which is the final resting-point. We have here one arsis and two theses.

It is evident that each of these compound beats, if isolated from its context, retains its own particular character. But if these compound beats are incorporated into the melodic synthesis of a whole piece, the part they then play is quite different. To deny this would be to deny the very existence of music!

Moreover, when you have carefully marked out the binary and ternary compound beats of a piece, do not think that your work is finished, even if it has been faultless. Your chant will then be correct, perhaps even smooth, but it will be cold and material, soulless and lifeless. You will, in fact, have left out what is most important. Too many scholae make this mistake. Remember that the primary beat maintains order and peace, so necessary to prayer, and the compound beats maintain the clearness and neatness of the movement. But the living touch, the profound significance of the work, its *raison d'être*, its power of supplication and its beauty — all these can be achieved only through composite rhythm and finally through the rhythm of the piece taken as a whole, through its "greater rhythm" (*le grand rythme*).

Sing, for example, Kyrie XI unevenly, then evenly, but paying attention only to the equality of the notes and to the succession of compound beats. Finally, sing it giving it its true rhythm and you will understand what I mean.

Let me remind the reader once and for all that in this constructive process, compound beats, because they depend completely on the ictus which governs them and of which they are only the complement, have the same relationship to each other as the ictuses which govern them. One may therefore apply the term arsic or thetic equally well to a compound beat or to its ictus.

TWO PRACTICAL QUESTIONS

In the interpretation of a Gregorian melody, how can the difference between an arsic and a thetic ictus be shown?

When the ictus occurs on the up-beat, it should be given more impetus and lightness, and quite often, though not necessarily, it should have slightly more strength. When the ictus is on the down-beat, it should be heavier, more restrained, and there should be slackening of the speed and often less strength.

We should like to mention here that there is an essential distinction between rhythm and stress, especially in an elementary rhythm. Although this distinction applies equally in a composite rhythm, we have to recognize the fact that quite often an ictus on the up-beat favors a slight increase in strength, and an ictus on the down-beat a slight softening of the tone. This point will be made clearer shortly when we speak of the dynamic line.

How can we decide whether an ictus is on an up-beat and arsic, or whether it is on a down-beat and thetic?

No exact and categorical answer to this question is possible, because the question itself is complex and because, in matters concerning art, it is difficult to formulate absolute rules. Only general directive guidance can be given, especially where two elements — melody and a Latin text — are involved, both of which have their own rights and between which conflict sometimes arises.

Theoretically, a melodic accent and the accent of the Latin word are by nature dynamically strong, whereas a melodic descent and non-accented Latin syllables (the penultimate syllable in a dactyl, and all final syllables) are by nature dynamically weak.

We can now draw the following conclusions: (1) in pure vocalization an ictus in a rising compound beat or those which are in a rising melody will be dynamically strong or arsic; an ictus on a descending compound beat or those which are in a descending melody will be dynamically weak or thetic. The general line of the melody will have to be taken into consideration, as well as the immediate context, and the shape or bias of the neum, etc.

(2) In chants with both words and melody we may find that the rhythm of words and melody agree, in which case an ictus on a rise in the melody which coincides with a tonic accent will certainly be arsic, and an ictus on a descent which coincides with a post-tonic syllable will certainly be thetic.

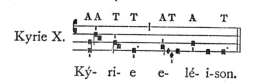

Kyrie X.

Ký- ri- e   e- lé- i-son.

Introït.

Sal-ve   sancta Pa- rens

Or, on the contrary, the rhythm of one may contradict that of the other. Each case must be judged on its own merits. Good taste and musical judgment will be required. In view of the ancient and traditional law of the subordination of the text to the melody, priority should be given to the latter when its line is well defined; otherwise the rthym of the words should be followed.

6. GREATER RHYTHM (LE GRAND RYTHME)

Composite rhythms unite to form groups, and these latter to form clauses, then phrases, and finally periods. Thus, link by link the unity of a whole piece is built up, and the synthesis in which rhythm essentially consists is obtained.

We thus come to the greater rhythm (*le grand rythme*), to something which is essentially alive, to movement on such a scale that it takes hold of all these elements, becomes part of them, and, in a series of increasingly comprehensive units, incorporates them step by step into the unity of the whole piece. All these small units — elementary rhythms, composite rhythms, groups, etc. — are merely fragments of this greater rhythm, on which their entire existence depends. They form only part of rhythm and, if I may say so, they are not themselves rhythm except by approximation. Their one objective is this greater rhythm, which alone gives them their *raison d'être* and even their respective cohesion.

But how is this rhythmic synthesis built up? In other words, how do composite rhythms combine to form groups, and groups to form clauses, and so on, since each of these units is in itself well defined, separate and, in a way, complete? The procedure is always the same. Each of the more complex units — groups, clauses, phrases — is constituted by the respective relationship formed between composite rhythms, then between groups, then between clauses, etc. This is a relationship of rise to fall, of arsis to thesis or, to use the language of ancient rhetoricians, of protasis to apodosis. *Each one has its musical and expressive centerpoint towards which everything tends and from which everything flows.* Within each one a hierarchy and a subordination of values is established which connects all these elements to one vital center, gives them their rightful place and blends them into the unity of the whole. What really counts here is the law of subordination.

Having thus secured unity within each group by the grading of composite rhythms around a centerpoint, you then unite these groups, grading them all around a principal accent so that they form a larger unit — the clause. In the same way clauses link together to form a phrase by means of a central accent to which all others will be subordinated. Finally, by treating phrases in the same way you will build up the unity of the whole piece and reach the final synthesis, i.e., that which does in fact constitute "rhythm."

If it should be asked how this subordination can make itself felt in practice at every step of the synthesis, the answer is a simple one: *by a dynamic* (stressed) *line based on the melodic line.*

7. THE DYNAMIC LINE

Let us begin with a general statement. Although the rhythmic ictus is entirely independent of stress and, in an elementary rhythm, may be either on the up-beat or on the down-beat, on rise or on fall, it does not follow that stress is in any way outside the realm of interpretation. Far from it. At this stage of our analysis it must be looked upon as indispensable, for it is stress which, by giving the whole phrase warmth and vivid coloring, underlines the phrase's unity. Unity between the various clauses and phrases can only be established by stress, which thus allows for the subordination of all else to the one central accent of which we have spoken. Without this uniting dynamic link, groups, clauses and phrases remain isolated from each other and are merely juxtaposed. This strikingly illustrates the extreme importance of the dynamic line in the musical interpretation of Gregorian chant.

The melodic line will, moreover, be above all the guiding factor in establishing the dynamic line. It is the melody which determines the various levels in the architecture of sound, and for a perfect interpretation it is the melody which must be followed step by step.

The interpreter's first task will be one of self-effacement. In considering the work to be interpreted, he must add nothing of his own, for this would be to betray the work and, in most cases, would lessen its value. Be it said in passing that herein lies the explanation of so many miserable failures. The interpreter is not, however, thereby freed from all personal mental effort, but his aim must be limited to discovering by every possible means the meaning of the work to be interpreted and what the composer intended. He will have to put aside his own taste and habits and especially his pre-conceived ideas whenever he feels that these run counter to the work itself of which it is his mission to give a true expression. If he is an artist he will still find plenty of scope for using his own per-sonal gifts.

Once again I repeat that it is the melodic line which will most surely reveal what he seeks. There is undoubtedly a close relation-ship between the ascending and descending melodic inflections and what I like to call the interior inflections of the soul. A melodic ascent is the expression of effort and increasing life, of expansion and joy; a melodic descent, on the contrary, is synonymous with gradual relaxation, moving towards an end.

It follows, and I think all musicians will agree with me, that a melodic rise should usually be sung with a crescendo and a melod-ic descent with a decrescendo. I say "usually" because there may be and are, in fact, exceptions to this rule. The melodically highest compound beat in each unit is normally the centerpoint of its unit. These centerpoints form a hierarchy of melodic summits which of themselves bring about a hierarchy of clauses.

In other words, the dynamic line must be based on the melodic line, which it follows step by step and of which it adopts every curve. All the smaller units must be allowed to keep their particu-lar rhythmic and dynamic character which will be incorporated into the whole. Thus, the slightest melodic ascent will, in practice, be accompanied by a correspondingly slight crescendo, and the slightest melodic descent by an appropriate decrescendo.

Let us complete the previous examples in accordance with what has just been said.

Kyrie X.

Ky- ri- e   e- lé- i-son.

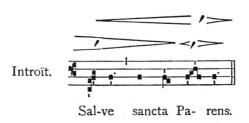

Introït.

Sal-ve   sancta Pa- rens.

We see here, realized, in practice, the interior unity of each group and the union of groups into clauses, etc., each of these units being centered around the highest compound beat.

I must add that these dynamic changes — which, of course, are always as gentle, discreet, and devoid of violent contrasts as the melodic line is itself pure and serene — should normally be accompanied by equivalent changes in the tempo, which should slacken and quicken continuously and be always in a state of flux. Anything rigid or artificial which might remain because too much attention has been given to the primary beat is thus obviated. This possible rigidity has, of course, already been tempered by the primary beat's function in both the compound beat and in the composite rhythm.

Thanks to its dynamic and quantitative suppleness and to the grading of all the elements involved, the melody takes on a warm and vivid color and its interpretation comes near to perfection. It combines the firmness of precision with a lively flexibility.

I believe that this detailed analysis of the melodic line should be constantly practiced. If it is neglected the results will be a rendering which may be correct but can hardly be good. It will remain material, fail to interpret the text, and thereby miss its objective and be unworthy of God's service.

8. CHIRONOMY

We have now reached the summit of the rhythmic synthesis and the end of the technical rules properly so-called. We must nevertheless say a few words about chironomy or the science of conducting choirs by gesture, which deservedly holds such an important place in Dom Mocquereau's teaching. True, it adds nothing to the synthesis which we have just outlined; it merely translates it, makes it perceptible, and provides valuable, indeed almost indispensable help in realizing it.

Chironomy, if all we have said is correct, can only be a plastic translation into space of melodic rhythm. This means that it is closely bound up with the rhythmical analysis of each piece, which, as we have said, it translates in gesture. There is an undoubted connection between musical rhythm and the rhythm of life, and since musical rhythm is but a manifestation of the rhythm of life or its translation into sound, this fact alone goes to show the importance of chironomy. The more the body is associated with musical rhythm, the better is this rhythm likely to be felt and rendered. The voice will faithfully reproduce what the gesture indicates, provided of course that the chironomy has the required qualities of being well defined and flexible. If these qualities are missing, then it can only do serious harm and should be omitted. I need not dwell here on the various movements which indicate an elementary rhythm or the thesis and arsis of a composite rhythm. Each arsis is translated by a clockwise circle of the hand, and each thesis by an undulating downward curve from left to right.

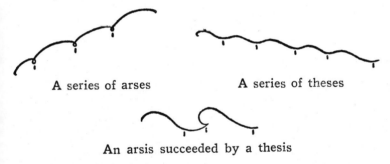

A series of arses   A series of theses

An arsis succeeded by a thesis

Detailed information can be found in the various textbooks on Plainsong. In this brief survey of the subject I shall confine myself to drawing the reader's attention to the following qualities that are of outstanding importance if chironomy is to serve a useful purpose.

Clearly defined movement

This is the most important quality and what follows is required. (a) In an elementary rhythm the gesture must show quite clearly the exact place of the rhythmic ictus, which is always at the very lowest point of the curve, whatever its shape. In other words, the curve must never continue to descend, in however small a degree,

after the ictus has been reached. (b) In a composite rhythm the
very shape of the curve, whether circular or undulating, should
show the arsic or thetic nature of the ictus within the synthesis of
the group or phrase. (c) Gestures should be so clear and distinct
as to make arsis and thesis easily recognizable. Too often choirmasters' gestures are vague and altogether useless.

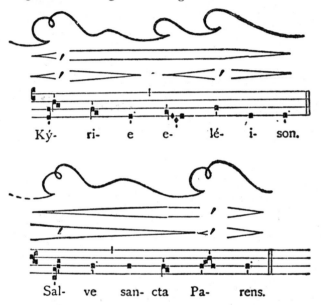

Thus used, chironomy becomes the exact and perfect picture of
the rhythmic synthesis of a piece and the crowning feature of all
we have been considering.

Flexibility

Chironomy must be able to follow all the fluctuations of free
rhythm with ease. That is why the modern "time beat," so often unsatisfactory even for music with a fixed measure, is far too rigid
to be used for freely alternating binary and ternary measures, or
to indicate resting-points which are, for the most part, soft and
light. This explains Dom Mocquereau's adoption of a less material
chironomic line, which, while both clearly defined and supple, was,
moreover, based on man's natural gesture.

In making these chironomic gestures careful attention should be given to the following: (a) to round them off as much as possible by keeping the arm from shoulder to finger tips supple and flexible; (b) to avoid any abrupt, stiff, mechanical, or angular movements; (c) to proportion their amplitude and energy to the degree of importance of arsis or thesis. A soft arsis — and one meets them — should obviously be distinguished from others by more restraint and delicacy and should be shown by the hand or fingers rather than by the whole arm or forearm. We thus have at our disposal a great hierarchy of gestures for every possible melodic, dynamic, and rhythmical contingency. (d) The conductor must not be afraid, should the need arise, even if the piece is in full swing, to change from broad phrasing to the most elementary chironomy in which, for instance, the compound beats are divided into two's and three's. This should be done when there is any sign of weakening on the part of the singers, or when they hesitate or hurry, or even when some small mark of expression needs to be made clearer and would not be shown by a broader gesture.

Chironomy is of real value in conducting choirs. It enables conductors to get a ready response as soon as the singers are sufficiently trained and are able to grasp the finer shades of interpretation. But it is no less valuable in providing training in rhythm for the individual, particularly in developing the habit of gentle descents, well-rounded summits, and well-blended compound beats. This training must not, however, be merely external and conventional. For this reason it is an excellent practice for choirmasters to train their singers in chironomy as far as is possible and to get them to make the movements of the chironomy as they sing.

I must point out, for the last time, that chironomy requires delicate handling. If well done, it is excellent; if badly done, it will on the contrary only perplex singers and even hamper them. This applies to whole choirs as well as to the individual.

The best results can be obtained only by persevering and methodical effort on the part of both conductor and singers, whose aim should be nothing short of the highest.

B. Rules on Style

We have now reached the summit of the rhythmic synthesis properly so called. The rules we have given, if well understood and put into practice, would suffice, no doubt, to produce a work of art and a rendering which comes very near to perfection. Yet, to remedy the defect of dryness and to give to the chant that musical and interior quality so important to its religious value something more is necessary. To the technical rules on rhythm those on style must be added. These are nearly as important as those on rhythm, if we include under style all the different procedures that help to give the chant its mellowness and weave around the rhythmic framework a veil which in no way diminishes its clarity, but softens anything sharp or angular in its outline.

One could expatiate endlessly on this question. Among many points which deserve to be mentioned, I shall name only a few particularly important ones which are of constant application.

1. LEGATO

Legato is one of the characteristics of Gregorian art, which is, above all, *prayer* and, as such, abhors anything which disturbs recollection and peace. There should therefore be no staccato, or hacked-out passages, no frequent breaks, especially at the small bars, but always a flowing "line"; this uninterrupted line follows the melodic line itself, which remains the supreme guide in all that concerns interpretation.

If we look carefully at the melody, we find in it nothing that jars, no syncopation, no big intervals. Very often — we might say most often — the melody moves by intervals of a second. Intervals of a third do occur; intervals of a fourth are far less frequent. Fifths are used with still more reserve, sixths are extremely rare, and there are no sevenths or octaves. (I speak of the compositions of the golden age of Plainsong.)

In singing these melodies, great care should be taken to maintain this legato. It was obviously in the minds of those who composed them and was for them an unquestionable and normal part of their interpretation. Dom Mocquereau liked to illustrate this point by referring to the cello which he had played in his youth.

We have already given the rules on the internal unity of compound beats, on the almost spiritual quality of accents, on the discretion of the dynamic line, and we shall have more to say about the softness of high notes — all will help to give us this precious legato. Nevertheless, for the choirmaster it must remain a matter of constant concern. He must also remember that legato should never revent the following: (a) the clear articulation of consonants, which is one of the indispensable qualities of all vocal music, whether ancient or modern. In a laudable attempt at securing legato, it is not unusual for singers to neglect this primary law concerning the clear pronunciation of syllables and especially of consonants, without which the text becomes unintelligible. Meanwhile, the singing, completely devoid of firmness and rhythm, degenerates into a sort of shapeless and sentimental hash which is entirely out of keeping with the spirit of Gregorian art.

(b) The clear distinction of verbal or melodic groups, about which we shall have more to say.

2. THE LIGHTNESS OF HIGH NOTES

Here, too, is a principle to which there can be practically no exception. This simple device, as musicians themselves have noticed, contributes greatly to giving the chant a religious character, so much does it imply the effacement of the person, the self, before Him to whom and for whom one is singing.

But it should be understood that I refer to lightness, not to weakness, the two are very different. Beware especially of singing top note mezzo-forte like a soft murmur. This top note is usually the true centerpoint, the keystone of the edifice, towards which everything tends. It should, therefore, be approached with a crescendo, as if it were to be sung with strength. It is only at the precise moment of emission that the voice, instead of attacking it loudly, harshly, materially, alights on it with gentleness and with some restraint, while allowing it to retain its full mellowness. What must be avoided is anything of an aggressive or angular character, as this would destroy the function of this high note, which, as Dom Mocquereau judiciously remarks, belongs not only to the ascent but quite as much to the descent which it has to prepare. There is thus nothing about it to suggest a sharp peak. It can be compared to the romanesque arch and, like it, is rounded in shape.

The melodic accent is above all a center of attraction. Accentuation, whether verbal or melodic, in our opinion, consists far more in the *preparation of the accent* than in the actual emission of the accented syllable or note. The accented syllable attracts to itself in a crescendo all that precedes it; then, having played its part, it is assimilated into what follows, and, like the summit of a roman-

esque vault, it blends the two slopes of sound into a harmoniou
whole. We have here a new and unexpected application of th
axiom: *Accentus anima vocis.*

To sum up. We have to guard against two extremes: singing thi
high note too loudly or, on the contrary, making it the weak ending
of a decrescendo. The best, as usual, is to adopt a middle course
which is to tend towards the high note in a true crescendo, tem
pered and softened at the exact moment of attaining it, making
the high note the luminous expansion, as it were, of the melodi
ascent.

It is this law concerning melodic summits which can perhap
give us the secret of how rightly to interpret the tonic Latin accent
This accent is itself the melodic summit of the word and ensure
cohesion and unity by the light it radiates on ante-tonic and post
tonic syllables: *anima vocis.* Rather than attack this high note i
a material fashion, prepare for it by a crescendo and hold back th
voice only at the very moment of its emission so that it may retair
strength as well as the gentleness derived from its spiritua
character.

In practice, a melodic summit and a tonic accent are much alike
Read through the fine passages in the *Nombre Musical* [7] in which
having established the nature and prerogatives of the tonic accent
Dom Mocquereau draws attention to the following practica
consequences:

> Great care must be taken to reach the accented syllable by
> a gentle ascent, by a moderate and careful crescendo, increas
> ing as the melody rises and proportioned according to th
> number of the ante-tonic syllables.

> Having reached the summit, anything hard or unexpected
> any vocal outburst on the top note must be avoided. Let u
> never forget: acuity is always the first and the most spiritua
> of the accent's qualities, and stress, which is of a more mate
> rial nature and over which even lightness takes precedence
> holds the last place.

> The turning point of the two slopes requires careful treat
> ment and should not form a sharp angle but a gracefully
> rounded, light, melodic curve. On the opposite side of th
> slope, the dynamic line bends downwards and, like the mel
> ody, comes gently to rest on the last syllable.

[7] *Nombre Musical,* t. II, pp. 237 and 240.

In the above passage for the verbal unity of the word the melodic unity of the phrase might be substituted. And if for the words "accent" or "accented syllable" you substitute "high notes," which are also the "musical accent" of the phrase, you will then have discovered the right manner of treating both melodic summits and Latin accents.

I quote once again from Dom Mocquereau: "When you reach the summit of this vault of sound, avoid the angular ogive, and seek rather the full romanesque arch; round off the outline." Then, quoting Dom Pothier, he adds: "Avoid hammering out the accented syllable, crushing it by weighty pressure, retarding its movement (unless to give elasticity) or slowing it down by any swelling of the voice." It is, in my opinion, very important to follow this rule if the Gregorian melody is to retain its true character. It applies always, even if the high note is ictic and even if it is the first note of a pressus or coincides with a tonic accent; and it applies equally to psalm cadences and to ornate chant. Sing, for example, Kyrie XI, the *propter magnam* of Gloria IX, the *Sanctus* and the *Benedictus* of Mass IX, the mediants of the eighth and third modes, etc.

3. VERBAL OR MELODIC "DISTINCTIONS"

For a complete understanding of the piece to be sung, this point is of special importance and pertains to verbal or musical diction. It consists in drawing close together those verbal or musical elements which belong to one another and making them distinct from others, even if this is not indicated in the musical notation. Or, to put it differently, it consists in *not* grouping together elements which logically should be dissociated.

Take the text *Hosánna in excélsis*. Short as it is, it contains nevertheless two parts: *Hosánna* and *in excélsis*. These should therefore be slightly separated from one another: *Hosánna — in excélsis*, and not sung as *Hosannaine — xcelsis*. Likewise in the psalm *Dixit Dominus*, the words *sede — a dextris meis*, and not *sedea — dextris meis*.

The danger exists especially when a word begins on a long note. If one were not careful, such a note might easily sound as if it were the thesis of what preceded, and therefore the end of the preceding word. Take, for example, the words *ampléctere Maríam* from the

antiphon *Adorna*, sung in procession on February 2, which one too
often hears as *amplecterema — riam.*

This rule applies equally in pure vocalizations, quite apart from
any verbal text. The melody is sometimes made up of theme
which answer one another, are in opposition to one another, com
plete each other, etc. Look, for instance, at the words *in aetérnur*
of the Gradual for Septuagesima, or at the jubilus of the Allelui
Loquebantur for Whit Monday. The themes must stand out clearly
otherwise all is confusion in which sounds have lost their meaning
The various levels of the melodic structure then become unrecog
nizable and its very basis is undermined. Plainsong is as muc
music as it is a verbal text, and each of these two elements has
right to be respected.

There is, moreover, no need to lengthen in any way the last not
or syllable of a first section, or to make it ictic. It can perfectly wel
remain on the up-beat. This is merely a matter of logical dissocia
tion, which can be shown by a slight break in the sound or rathe
by an almost imperceptible slowing down before the melod
starts off again. It is something in the nature of the *"tempus vacan*
. . . *inane quid"* that Quintilian required between each word i
speech.

Nothing in this is contrary to the principle of the subordinatio
of words to melody or to the rhythmical mechanism properly s
called, since such breathing spaces are common usage in a
music.

And here is an opportunity for making an important statement
IN SINGING, ONE'S AIM IS NOT TO EMIT A SERIES OF SOUNDS NOR T
CONFORM TO MUSICAL THEORY BUT TO EXPRESS AN IDEA OR A SENTI
MENT. MUSIC IS A LANGUAGE, OF A SPECIAL KIND, NO DOUBT; BU
NEVERTHELESS TRULY A LANGUAGE, AND AS SUCH, IF IT IS TO B
UNDERSTOOD, IT MUST BE INTERPRETED WITH INTELLIGENCE. FO
THIS, EVERY DETAIL WITHIN THE SYNTHESIS MUST BE GIVEN IT
PROPER VALUE, JUST AS IT WOULD BE IN A PUBLIC SPEECH. SINGIN
IS AN ACT OF THE MIND AND NOT MERELY A VOCAL EXERCISE. I
MUST BE SOMETHING HUMANLY PERFORMED, *humano modo*, AN
IT MUST BRING INTO ACTION ALL THE VITAL FORCES OF THE INTEF
PRETER.

Nor can Plainsong be exempt from such requirements. To
often people are satisfied when they have applied material rule
and seem unaware of the fact that these very rules are ordaine
to another end!

This would be a well-chosen moment, if one had the time, t

emind the reader of establishing — by breathing spaces, pauses, etc. — a hierarchy between the various units which make up musical language: groups, clauses, phrases, without which, clearly, no synthesis is possible. The various chant manuals give the required information. It should, however, be noted that a certain elasticity is sometimes needed in assessing the time-value of the bar-line. The usual rules, which are based on common sense, should not be too rigidly kept; interpretation may be given a wide margin.[8]

I may be allowed just two brief comments on breathing spaces and group endings, which often give rise to obviously exaggerated interpretation. In the past, breath was taken anywhere. To breathe nowhere would seem to be the fashion today. In either case the result is exactly the same: the structural outline of the composition becomes unrecognizable. Although collective breathing at every quarter-bar line may not be desirable, there are many cases where this is permissible. The whole choir should, I think, normally take breath at the half-bar, but on the value of the doubled note preceding the half-bar. Breath taken on the value of a doubled note need not necessarily break up the unity of the phrase. It would be different if one or two beats of complete silence were added. It is thus quite easy to distinguish and grade the different units: simple group (quarter-bar line), more developed groups or clauses (half-bar lines), phrases (whole-bar lines), and thus a complete synthesis emerges of itself.

Special mention must also be made of quarter-bar lines preceded by a podatus or a clivis with horizontal episema. The great majority of choirs, to avoid over-lengthening the second note, reduce it to the value of a sixteenth note and literally jump on to the beginning of the following group, to the great detriment of musical sense, common logic, and peace, which is at once disturbed by the inevitable impression of a jolt. The singers, no doubt, mean well, but they go too far and the result is unsatisfactory. In such cases the necessity for a clear "distinction" is evident. Time must be taken to sing the two slightly lengthened notes with due care and to detach them from what follows by an almost imperceptible delay before beginning the next group. The impression thus created is that the choir is quite at ease and singing naturally, and nothing could be more favorable to the spirit of prayer.

[8] Cf. "Les barres de la notation grégorienne et la ponctuation musicale," *Rev. Grég.* (1948), pp. 183–191.

4. FLEXIBILITY OF THE TEMPO

In spite of what is stated in a number of textbooks on the chant there is no set pace for plainsong in general; neither is there any special pace for each of the various kinds of pieces, i.e., one speed for Introits, another for Graduals, Offertories, etc. Plainsong is music and much too subtle an art to lend itself to anything so rigid. The truth is that each piece, of whatever category, requires its own pace, the pace which will produce the required effect.

Taken separately, neither the words nor the melody can determine this pace. Both text and melody must be considered together, interpreted one by the other, each in relation to the other. Generally speaking, the melody seems to play the principal part and more particularly, the mode in which it is written.

The tempo varies from one piece to another, but it can and often should vary within the same piece from one part to another. This is particularly noticeable in long pieces such as responsories, Graduals, Offertories, in which one should not be afraid of changing the speed as soon as the need is felt, at the same time avoiding too abrupt contrasts. It is, in fact, rare to find a melody with any neumatic development that does not require some such change in its pace. But the melody need not even be very long, since the shortest antiphons may lend themselves to delicate fluctuations in tempo which contribute so much to the understanding of a piece.

If we bear in mind the slight slackening in speed which usually precedes a big cadence (this slowing down should not be exaggerated but should be in keeping with the character of the piece) and more especially if we remember what has been said about variations in speed brought about by the slightest ascent or descent in the melody, we shall see that the tempo is always truly flexible. Any objection based on the material rigidity of a chant made up of strictly equal notes is thereby once and for all disproved. There is truly nothing more flexible than this chant, with its many scarcely perceptible shades of expression both as regards rhythm and melodic and modal line. It is indeed impossible to imagine any more suitable medium for translating the complex feelings of the human soul.

Finally, it should be noted that this flexibility in tempo does not in any way conflict with the great principle of the indivisibility of the primary beat. The equality in time-value of the notes is, as we have already said, relative and not absolute. Their duration will naturally vary according to the tempo adopted, automatically expanding and contracting with it. But these almost imperceptible shades of expression have nothing in common with the subdivisions of a primary beat. They are nevertheless very real and every musician should be aware of them.

5. THE HORIZONTAL EPISEMA

Gregorian notation contains a great number of expressive neums. Some of these have been retained in the Vatican edition, e.g., the quilisma and the liquescent note. Others are shown only in the Solesmes editions, e.g., the horizontal episema and the salicus, not to mention the oriscus, strophicus and liquescent punctum, reproduced only in the monastic books (Antiphonary, Office of the Dead and the Nativity).

I should have liked to dwell on the spiritual significance of these elements which are such powerful means of expression, but space forbids. I can only touch upon the subject and shall do no more than treat of horizontal episemas. It should be understood that what is said of these applies also in part, *positis ponendis*, to the quilisma and the salicus.

These signs are not, strictly speaking, signs of length but signs of expression, although, of course, they should be translated by a slight lengthening and softening of the note over which they are placed. They remain, nevertheless, above all, expression marks. Their function is to translate the infinite variety of feelings that surge up in the human heart. If they are to be considered as lengthening signs, which materially they are, then they are so only as a means of expression; their lengthening is not an end in itself but the means to an end.

In singing there is therefore no need to guard against emphasizing them, even if the effect should *seem* slightly exaggerated. I have noticed that most choirs, in their fear of overstressing them, reduce them so strictly to the conventional proportion that one is hardly aware of them. In a chant with notes of relatively equal length such as Gregorian chant, it is this expressive holding of notes that gives the melody both warmth and a spiritual quality.

Here is some practical and detailed advice on how to sing notes with the horizontal episema. The horizontal episema is only an expression mark. It does not therefore affect the rhythmical structure of a passage, and it leaves the rhythmical quality of the note which it marks unchanged.

a) In an elementary rhythm

If it marks a note on the up-beat, the note naturally remains on the up-beat and does not become an ictic note in any way; its fundamental lightness must therefore be respected. In such a case the note must on no account be doubled. The horizontal episema's function here is to emphasize the *élan* of the note by a discreet ritenuto as one would an accent on the up-beat, but more obviously. This is a delicate nuance but one which admirably brings out the idea to be expressed.

Ant.   Ecce   ancílla Dómini   Ant.   Rex pa-cí-ficus

The case is the same for the accent on *fru-* in the following antiphon *De fructu*. In all these examples asterisks mark the application of the principle we have been describing.

If, on the contrary, the horizontal episema is placed on an ictic note, as it most frequently is, the marked note naturally remains ictic and to its relative weight more length may well be added occasionally its value may even be doubled. There is no harm in this so long as the note keeps its expressive character. A slight minimum lengthening would give a flat, cold, lifeless impression and be far more likely to impede the flow of the melodic and rhythmic line.

Ant.   De fructu   ventris tu- i

The effect of the horizontal episema will, however, differ according to whether the ictus on which it is placed is arsic or thetic, and this brings us to the compound beat.

b) In a composite rhythm

If the horizontal episema is placed over an arsic ictus, it should in no way diminish its characteristic *élan* and impetus. The episema will, on the contrary, be the perfect means for giving this impetus

its full expressive value and will at the same time draw attention
to its prominent place in the general economy of the phrase. Care
should therefore be taken not to make it heavy, and it should keep
all its vitality and elasticity. The accent on *ven-* in the antiphon
De fructu is a case in point.

On a thetic ictus (syllables *tris tu-i*) the note which it covers is
naturally heavier and can be held even to the extent of doubling
its value. It has often a caressing quality which draws the mind to
loving contemplation of the idea expressed. It is certainly better to
exaggerate its length slightly than to skim over it. Here is an example from the paschal *Agnus Dei*:

qui tollis peccá-ta mundi

Theoretically speaking, the episema affects only the first note
of the clivis — this is an important point to which I can merely
draw attention here — but the second note also comes under its
influence. Moreover, the whole passage is here indirectly affected
by it: the words *peccáta mundi* acquire an incontestable gentleness and restraint and sense of confidence.

The horizontal episema is thus a shade of expression, which
means that its value is in no way mathematical but depends on
numerous factors based on no fixed rules. The interpreter will have
to choose the shade of color he thinks best for it. Speaking generally, it is best treated gently. It is an invitation, not to external
display, but to enter into one's soul and there to find the indwelling
Guest. It is one of the elements which greatly help to give our
Gregorian melodies their contemplative value.

c) On several consecutive neums

So far we have spoken only of cases where the horizontal episema covers a single note or two notes. If it should extend over a
whole long passage as, for example, on the *portávit* of the Response
Ecce vidimus for Maundy Thursday, or the *adoráte Dóminum* in
the Communion *Tollite hostias* for the eighteenth Sunday after
Pentecost, care should be taken not to hammer out each note. The
whole passage needs to be sung broadly, as though marked *can-
tando* or *allargando*.

d) On a lengthened torculus

We have to consider two cases here. Either the lengthened torculus is placed at cadences or it occurs within a group.

1) In the torculus of cadences, which occurs frequently in ornate chant and is merely an ornamental form of the corresponding syllabic cadence (■ · ■ ·) , the first note carries all the weight of the drop; the two others are merely its development and its complement, as in the compound beat (see p. 43). They are, therefore, basically lighter but they share in the general broadening and should be sung with a decrescendo.

2) In the middle of a melodic development the lengthened torculus is designed merely to guide the melodic and rhythmic stream towards the center to which it is tending. It might be called the "guiding torculus." It should, therefore, be sung with a gradual allargando and a crescendo.

6. ORDINARY NEUMS HAVE NO SPECIAL INFLUENCE ON STYLE

Apart from these neums of expression which figure only in the very earliest manuscripts of the tenth and eleventh centuries, what view can be taken of ordinary neums with no additional signs which are to be found in manuscripts of every period, including the earliest? In the following paragraph I shall refer to these alone and restrict myself entirely to the question of style.

Do ordinary neums, as such, have a direct influence on style? In other words, can they modify or overrule the delicate shades of expression which we have been at pains to describe in the preceding pages?

The answer is most emphatically NO. Style, like rhythm, moves freely among neums, which in themselves have no expressive character whatsoever. It is sometimes objected, when some particular nuance is asked for, that the neums "don't show anything." It would indeed be foolish to maintain that the neums say everything and that we need only follow them to attain perfection. They are, in fact, merely a very embryonic form of notation. They do not even indicate exact melodic intervals, nor do they give even the most essential of the multiple marks of expression required for the interpretation of the melody.

The neums of the books in actual use today are merely a stylistic typographical reproduction of the early neums of St. Gall. It is certain that these ancient neums were first and foremost an approximative system of melodic notation indicating, and that very roughly, *the succession of high and low notes and their legato over a single syllable.*

Neums are, therefore, first and foremost *melodic signs*; their rhythmic value takes only second place.[9] They have no dynamic value. There is no such thing as a "strong neum." There is moreover nothing surprising in this. Dom Mocquereau rightly observed that the old grammarians, who had at their disposal a whole arsenal of signs to punctuate the unfolding of a phrase or to underline subtle shades of expression, had none to indicate stress.[10] These were introduced by the Latin grammarians only in the sixth century. Even then the terms they used — *plus sonat*, etc. — were vague, and it requires some good will to recognize in them signs denoting stress. The so-called "stress" letters in the Sangallian manuscripts of the golden age are extremely rare.

We can learn a lesson from all this. We today give too much prominence to stress as a landmark in musical performance. This, at least, is our impression from the questions which are daily put to us. The art of the old musicians was much more delicate and consequently much more spiritual. Material strength was not their aim so much as expression, which is the soul's province. For them stress was not something rather brutal, perpetually renewed, but a warm, vivid coloring extending over the whole phrase and emphasizing its unity.

[9] In only slightly ornate chant, where the syllables are each given hardly more than two or three notes (e.g., the *Asperges me* and many of our *Glorias* etc.), the grouping of notes into two's and three's on one syllable normally corresponds with the grouping of compound beats, and thus the beginning of the neum coincides with the ictus. (The neums should, in such cases, be treated in the same way as compound beats of which they are a graphic representation. See p. 43.) But in melismatic passages, with long vocalizations, it would be rash to presume that the neums in themselves have a rhythmic character and that their first note necessarily indicates the place of the ictus. The ancient writers do not usually seem to have had such an idea in their minds.

For the same reason it is time we got rid of the legend of "the integrity of the neum" and "indivisibility of the neum." Once again, neums are merely melodic aggregates or a succession of notes sung on the same syllable which can be given various rhythmic subdivisions. The manuscripts bear witness to this over and over again. The rhythmic reality is not the neum but the *compound beat.*

[10] *Nombre Musical*, t. II, p. 154, footnote.

There is no need, therefore, as regards expression, to bother about what the neums do or do not indicate. *They were not created for that purpose.* The laws which govern stress and expression depend on the melodic line itself or on the accents of the words, and not on neums, which are merely forms of writing.

The dynamic strength of a neum thus depends neither on its shape nor on its name, but on its place in the melodic line or on the syllable on which it rests. Interpretation is thus undoubtedly liberated from many unjustifiable restrictions and gains unquestionably in flexibility and freedom of movement.

Contrary to a widespread opinion, the same applies to the pressus. It is no more a "strong neum" than any other. Composers have placed it on any degree of the scale and anywhere in the melodic line. We can at least say that no positive proof of its strength comes to us from antiquity. It is significant that most of the longer pieces of the Mass (Graduals, Alleluias, Tracts, Offertories) finish with a pressus. This marks the end of the long apodosic descent in which the melody, moving gradually more slowly, pauses for a last time before finally coming to rest. Any sudden increase of sound at this very point would be ridiculous. Music is a language which has a definite meaning as well as rights to defend.

The pressus is, in fact, very valuable rhythmically. By their natural weight these neums play a particularly important part in the architectural structure of the melody. Dom Mocquereau compared them to solid pillars on which the whole musical structure rests, but he assured me that he was referring to their *rhythmical* importance and not necessarily to their dynamic strength.[11] Because of our modern obsession with stress, the distinction between rhythm and stress needs to be kept in mind.

The same can be said of the bivirga, which is long but not necessarily stressed. In singing, these neums must be given their *full time-value*, which is that of two primary beats. They even need to be well emphasized, especially when there are a number of them, as often happens. One may be tempted to skim over them on the pretext that they may make the melody heavy, but they usually have the opposite effect. When sung in succession, long, shapeless phrases do produce an effect of heaviness. If bivirgas are given

---

[11] The distinction between a pressus and a strophicus is not one of stress but one of rendering. A pressus is a single sound held for two beats, whereas a strophicus implies the repercussion of each of the component sounds.

their clearly defined double value, then the performance will retain its full clarity and vigor. Their dynamic strength should be in keeping with their position in the development of the melodic and rhythmic line.

7. ADVICE CONCERNING THE FOLLOWING NEUMS

a) The pressus preceded by a single note on a new syllable

When a new syllable, with or without accent, is placed on a single note immediately preceding a pressus, it should be treated in the normal way. The ictus remains on the pressus and the note preceding the pressus is on the up-beat. This note on the up-beat should, however, be slightly amplified and rounded so that the voice may glide naturally and with a slight delay on to the pressus, which should be sung gently and without any suggestion of harshness.

Here are several examples taken from the Introit *Salve sancta parens*:

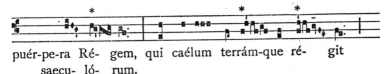

puér-pe-ra Ré- gem, qui caélum terrám-que ré- git
saecu- ló- rum.

If, as is the case here, the syllable is accented (RÉgem, saecuLÓ-rum, toRÁMque, RÉgit), there should be no "sliding over the accent" from the first note to the pressus. The place of the accent remains unchanged and is given its gentle emphasis which is characteristic of the Latin tonic accent given at the exact moment and on the note on which it occurs, that is, on the first note. It is really a kind of "accent on the up-beat" which must be given the same treatment as described on page 47. The four accents marked with an asterisk in the last example are actually sung in the same way as the accent on the up-beat of *cóelum*.

If the syllable is unaccented, the note on the up-beat obviously needs no special stress but should be very slightly broadened. In any case, the pressus itself should be sung softly.

This emphasis on the first note is necessary when the note is detached from the pressus and should be made even when the note is joined to the pressus in the form of a clivis or a podatus. This avoids a vertical drop which would be repugnant to good taste and a sense of style. The salicus usually requires the same treatment.

b) The climacus

This should never be sung hurriedly, especially if it is long. Quite often in the old manuscripts there are lengthening signs on the first note and even on all the notes. This is a precious indication and suggests a general principle. Here is an application of the beautiful old dictum: *Ascensiones pudicae, descensiones temperatae.* As always, we find here that sobriety and sense of proportion characteristic of Gregorian prayer.

c) Liquescent notes

These affect syllables which may be difficult to pronounce, such as diphthongs, and the conjunction of certain consonants. They are put as a warning sign and invite the singer to take the necessary time to pronounce everything properly, even should the theoretical equality of syllables suffer thereby.

Their normal length and strength should not be reduced, and like any other note they must be given their full rhythmic and dynamic value. Most often they even benefit from being slightly amplified.

8. THE OCCASIONAL BROADENING OF SINGLE BEATS

Gregorian art, like all music worthy of the name, can be given many shades of expression. It belongs to its own time and differs in its rhythm and modal system from classical and modern music. Yet when we consider its general interpretation, we find that it is subject to the same great laws as govern musical art of all times and all countries. There has been too great a tendency to isolate it. It has been looked upon as something unrelated to anything outside itself, whereas it is linked by the closest ties to all that has preceded and followed it.

Let us add some further aids to expression, some other legitimate ways of mitigating the strictness in time-value of the single beat. These will again show the flexible and truly spiritual character of the chant. I shall confine myself to brief indications which anyone will be free to develop.

a) Isolated notes between two lengthened notes

By "lengthened notes" I mean any note of which the value is greater than that of an ordinary primary beat, whether it be actually doubled (dotted notes, pressus, strophicus, notes with oriscus) or merely lengthened (notes with horizontal episema or before a quilisma).

These notes rank high in the rhythmical structure of the piece. Their importance tends forcibly to efface the single notes which are in their immediate vicinity and, so to speak, wedged between them. In Gregorian chant, and especially in ornate chant, there are many cases of isolated notes between lengthened ones. These isolated notes are often sung hurriedly and even reduced to the value of sixteenth notes. The melody then seems to move in leaps and jerks and gives an unpleasant impression of unsteadiness and lack of balance. This destroys the impression of plenitude and peace which are the very essence of Gregorian prayer.

Special care must be taken to give these single notes their full value as primary beats and even to broaden them a little. This does not mean that they themselves must be actually lengthened, but they should benefit from the surrounding atmosphere and be allowed to "breathe freely." This will at once enhance the meaning of a prayer.

The same applies to a single isolated note between two lengthened notes (the most frequent case):

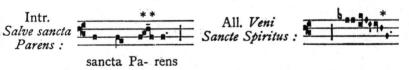

Intr. *Salve sancta Parens :*   sancta Pa- rens   All. *Veni Sancte Spiritus :*

It also applies in cases where there are two notes:

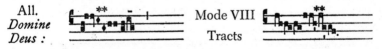

All. *Domine Deus :*   Mode VIII Tracts

Here is a characteristic example taken from the Alleluia *Adorabo* of the Dedication:

et confi-té-   bor

All the notes marked with an asterisk should be treated in the way just described. Where there are two notes, there is a compound beat of two notes and they should be treated as such (cf. page 43) and even slightly broadened. Try singing *et confitébor* both ways, first shortening, then slightly broadening the notes marked with an asterisk, and my meaning will be clear.

b) Wide descending intervals

The second last example (a formula of Mode VIII Tracts) introduces us to a new series requiring similar treatment. In the case of considerably wide descending intervals (fourths and fifths), any quick drop on to the lower note must be avoided, and for this reason it is better slightly to broaden the higher of the two notes.

Kyrie IV :   Kýri- e   e- léison.   Kyrie IX : Ký-ri- e

A drop in the melody should never give the impression of being vertical but should be rounded or curved. Gregorian art is like romanesque art and avoids sharp angles. There must be no yielding to a kind of attraction from below with a tendency to hasten the speed. Each note must be given its full time-value; this in itself will produce the right effect.

c) Melodic descents ending on a long note

In melodic descents moving either by conjoined or separated intervals and coming to rest on a long note (especially a pressus), one may easily be tempted to shorten the note before the long one; but it must be given its full time-value and even very slightly held back in discreet preparation for the cadence.

Allelúia
Ascension :   Alle- lú- ia

Although it applies more particularly to melodic descents, the same treatment can also be used for melodic ascents. As has already been said, a long note should never be attacked abruptly but must be approached with care.

d) Repeated notes on the up-beat

A repeated note on an up-beat must certainly not be heavy, but neither must it be shortened and treated as a sixteenth-note. The note should be slightly rounded, rather like an accent on the up-beat, but, of course, without any stress and as gently as possible.

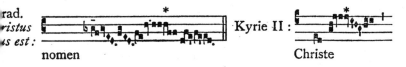

9. CONTINUITY OF LINE

Unity and life are qualities which are essential to any musical performance. They depend especially on two great factors: on rhythm, especially compound rhythm, and on the dynamic line. It is important not to split up the rhythm by frequent breaks but to allow it to develop in one continuous movement. In conclusion we shall give some further advice on how to achieve this unity and how to overcome some of the obstacles that stand in its way.

a) Group endings

The small bar-lines which mark the ends of groups seem to present the most serious obstacle to rhythmical unity. To achieve unity within each group is relatively easy to anyone at all musical. To maintain this unity when passing from one group to another is much more difficult; yet, if unity is lacking, the performance is reduced to a series of new beginnings.

Dom Mocquereau, to whom this question was a matter of concern, has written about it at some length in the second volume of his *Nombre Musical* (pp. 597–605). There, speaking of the unity of the phrase, he devotes a whole paragraph to what he calls the "articulation link," which acts between groups and clauses exactly at the point of their junction.

Here are three excellent ways suggested by Dom Mocquereau to provide this link: (1) the compound beat, which within its own unity embodies the end of the first group and the beginning of the next one; (2) the composite rhythm, which joins two groups by treating the beginning of the new group as a thesis and thus making it depend on a previous arsis; (3) where no breath is taken the *mora vocis* links the two groups to one another by a crescendo (or maybe a decrescendo) on the final note of the first group. This final note acts as a pivot or joint through which the living current of melody and rhythm passes and is transmitted from one clause to another.

To continue the subject of the *mora vocis*, it must start gently since it is the conclusion of a small unit. While it is being held, the note should be given the slight emphasis required to lead up to what follows. The whole must sound natural and unaffected. Any abrupt crescendo would be quite out of place.

This preparing for what is to follow by a very slight crescendo or insistence on the last notes even before the end of a first group is a commendable but delicate process and needs to be done with great care.

b) Sustained notes

Here is another obstacle to "continuity of line" and to vitality in the rendering. It is a very real obstacle because sustained notes occur frequently and because there is too often lack of attention on the part of singers. These notes which occur in the course of a phrase are the various "long notes" of which we have already spoken.

By the way they are sung, sustained notes often immobilize the melody and give an impression of halts and interruptions in the rhythmic flow. But they too must take part in the life of the group or phrase by tending towards what follows in an appropriate crescendo or decrescendo. In other words, there must be no immobilized notes or halts but held notes that are "on the move."

Neither must there be sustained notes that are merely "in juxtaposition." This is often heard when two doubled notes follow each other, as, for example, a podatus or a clivis in which both notes are dotted. The movement must be felt to pass from one note to the other, gliding from the one into the other. This is a consequence of the very nature of the rhythmic ictus, which is merely a touching-point in the melody's movement, except, of course, when it is the final ictus.

And so the danger exists not only at the ends of groups but is present throughout the melodic discourse every time a lengthened note appears; and lengthened notes are very numerous. It is therefore a point which requires constant attention.

c) Cadences in alternating chants

For the same reason, in alternating chants (hymns, Kyrie, Gloria, Credo) care must be taken to avoid making exaggerated rallentandos at each of the cadences, thus treating them as final cadences and giving an impression that the end of the piece has been reached. Nothing could be more detrimental to the unity of the whole, that great law which governs rhythm. It is only quite at the end of a piece (the last line of a hymn, the last *Kyrie*, the *Amen* of a Gloria and a Credo) that the cadence may be really broadened in an appropriate manner.

Everywhere, except at the ending, only slight broadening will be needed, just enough to emphasize the musical cadence and to prevent its being hard and material (another fault against which we must be on our guard).

All this applies equally and perhaps above all to psalmody, notably to those psalm-endings on a clivis or a podatus. Interruption of the movement at the end of each verse would inevitably destroy that great rocking movement which is so characteristic of psalmody and such an aid to contemplation. It will suffice if two full beats are given to each of the dotted notes of the podatus or clivis.

d) The "horizontal" melodic line

Sometimes the melody itself seems to stand still. It has already been said, and the point stressed, that the melodic line with its ascending and descending curves, expressing the "interior curves of the soul," almost automatically brings about variations in emphasis and tempo, establishes a hierarchy between the various parts, and by their respective accents makes them converge towards unity.

Sometimes, however, the melodic line seems to develop on a horizontal plane, hardly leaving a reciting note, around which it seems content to undulate. Let us quote, for example, the Introits *In medio* of the Common of Doctors; *Misericordia Domini* of the second Sunday after Easter; *In voluntate tua* of the twenty-first Sunday after Pentecost; the Offertory *Domine convertere* of the Sunday after Corpus Christi; the Communion *Tu es Petrus*, etc.

How should they be sung? How can the continuity of the melodic line be combined with an impression of life? On closer examination one always finds a melodic accent, a point of attraction however unobtrusive, towards which the movement of the melody can be directed.

Thus in the Introit *In medio* there is a first small crescendo toward *-clé* of *ecclésiae*; then a second, more pronounced crescendo towards *éjus*. This first phrase, which is almost *recto tono*, is merely a getting ready and a starting-point for the marked ascent of the second phrase: *et implévit*. It will then be easy to make a beautiful and very gradual crescendo from the intonation right up to *eum* in the second phrase, which dominates the whole of this truly magnificently balanced piece.

e) Repetitions of the same theme

In long vocalizations, especially those of Alleluias, it is not unusual to find a repetition of the same melodic theme. These repetitions must never be treated as an echo. This is a procedure of doubtful taste which roughly interrupts the dynamic development of the phrase and breaks into the melody's rhythmical line. In addition, it aims at effect for effect's sake, transforms the rendering into a concert performance, and thereby radically destroys the impression of prayer.

But, although this use of the echo effect should be inexorably banned, it does not at all follow that the repetition of a theme should be a mere reproduction of what preceded it. This also would be detrimental to the "line," to the progressive and steady trend towards a center, of which we have so often spoken and from which the unity of a piece is derived. The repetition should be made with either a crescendo or a decrescendo (the latter is a very different thing from an echo) according to the requirements of each case and the taste of the interpreter.

It is very difficult to formulate any general rule. Here is what would seem wise to suggest: (1) If the repetition forms part of a general line of ascent, it should certainly be interpreted with a crescendo.

All. *Justus germinabit :*

2) If, on the contrary, it is placed in a long descending progres-
ion, it may be sung either with a decrescendo, in view of the
eneral melodic line, or, if advisable, with a crescendo, because
f the possibly implied insistence on the composer's mind.

All. *Domine Deus :*

3) In many cases the general line is so skilfully varied that it
ecomes difficult to judge exactly in what way it is evolving. In
uch cases the interpreter is free to use his own judgment.

Generally speaking, it would seem that a crescendo is always
ossible.

) Final cadences

A final cadence most often requires considerable broadening.
3ut we must be on our guard against laying down hard and fast
ules for so flexible an art.

We are dealing with music. The general speed, the expression
nd intensive coloring of each piece require appropriate treatment
nd so does the final cadence. It will be more or less broadened
ccording to the general character of the piece or the nature of the
inal formula chosen by the composer. This is really a matter of
aste. There are even pieces which, according to very clear indi-
ations in the manuscripts themselves, end without any slackening
f speed, as, for example, the Introits *Hodie scietis* for the vigil of
he Nativity, the *Omnes gentes* for the seventh Sunday after Pente-
ost.

This shows that here as elsewhere the interpreter is bound by
10 strict law but is quite free to follow his own inspiration. Never-
heless, it remains true that in short antiphons as well as in the
nost ornate pieces final cadences require in varying degrees a
ertain amount of breadth.

) Holding the final note

Lastly, the final note itself requires special care. Over and above
ts gentleness, two conditions govern the way in which it is ap-
roached and held, and these suffer no exception:

1) The final note must not be emitted hurriedly or allowed to drop clumsily. The preceding note should be held·back a little and the final note itself sung with a very slight delay, as if it had to pause before alighting.

2) Once emitted it should be given its full value since it marks the end of the entire melodic, modal, and rhythmic movement of the piece, which here finds its achievement and conclusion. The same holds good in ornate and in syllabic chant or in psalmody itself. The note must not, however, be indefinitely prolonged. It should last for *two whole beats* up to, but excluding, the following ictus, which is the conclusion.

These two rules are very important. They establish the cadence and leave us in that atmosphere of perfect serenity in which interior contemplation, the supreme object of sung prayer, may pursue its way in silence.

CONCLUSION

Gregorian Art As Prayer

In spite of its shortcomings, this treatise will, we hope, give the reader some idea of the beauty and flexibility of Plainsong. If space allowed, much more could be written about its interpretation. Material for this is not lacking. It has been said that a technique of mathematical precision should never be allowed to oppose the suprarational exigencies of the music or a thorough understanding of the words; neither should it conflict with that sum total of imponderable shades of expression which we call style.

What has been said about the primary beat remains the basis of our teaching, just as it was the basis of ancient rhythm. From it the melody derives firmness, and can, at the same time, lend itself most happily to a wide range of expression. Music, it has often been said, is the most subtle of all the arts, the one that sinks most deeply into the soul and can best translate its highest aspirations. There is certainly no music more flexible than the Gregorian melody at every level of its rhythmic and modal structure, as well as in its composition and inspiration.

As an art it ranks high among the arts, but it is much more than an art. It goes far beyond music, which becomes merely a means to an end. It is above all a prayer, better still, *the* prayer of the Catholic Church, which here attains its full expression. It is, therefore, something pertaining to the soul and stands on a higher plane, like the entire liturgy, of which it forms a part and from which it cannot be separated. It is a form of spirituality, a way of reaching up to God and of leading souls to God. It is supremely efficacious as a means of sanctification and of apostolate.

That is why it must be treated with infinite reverence in its technique and its spirit. In its rhythm and in its modality it excludes anything which might impair its firmness and nobility, or the tranquil and harmonious flow of the melody. We find no leading-notes, chromatics, wide intervals, syncopation, and no

divisibility of the primary beat. Neither do we find anything whic
might materialize the melody such as a fixed measure, angularit
or strong beats. All these would stand in the way of recollectio
and prayer. Instead, we are given an exquisite impression of sobr
ety and strength, serenity, restraint, perfect balance together wit
freedom and flexibility. The chant thus wonderfully translates th
attitude of the creature in the presence of his God, an attituc
of reverence and adoration, of humility, confidence and dee
tenderness, of faith, hope and charity.

These qualities belong to Plainsong and must be preserved at a
costs. The rules concerning technique and style will each in the
own way contribute to this end. None can be ignored becaus
Plainsong does not tolerate mediocrity. The rules of techniqr
assure order and peace, unity and life; the rules of style temp
what might be too rigid or mechanical in the application of th
former and introduce that immaterial element which is so muc
in keeping with the spiritual language of prayer.

This is an art which is both divine and human — divine becaus
of its supernatural inspiration and that sweet and lovely odor
sanctity which breathes in all its melodies; and at the same tin
profoundly human by its musical structure and in the response
finds in simple, upright souls eager for truth.

Such is the art of Plainsong as it emerges from the close ar
impartial study of its paleographical, musical, and philologic
sources. It has been restored to us by the patient research carrie
on unremittingly for over a century at Solesmes, under the initi
and vigorous direction of Dom Mocquereau.

Art and prayer: these two aspects of the chant are closely boun
together and are complementary to one another. Each has its ow
exigencies. In this survey my aim has been to give rules for th
musical interpretation of the chant. Although these are necessar
and even serve the purpose of bringing out the fundamental
religious character of Gregorian art, they are in themselves inad
quate. Other qualities are required of the interpreter which ai
just as essential. They are those very qualities which the Gregoria
melody so perfectly translates: true humility, faith, and love.

It is only when all these conditions are fulfilled that the Gregor
an melody can produce in souls its blessed fruits of peace an
sanctification. For those who give themselves up to it with humilit
and love it can become not only an endless source of profoun
artistic joy, but also a wonderful instrument of spiritual educatic
and of fruitful apostolate.